Strings & IVORY

Music Reference Guide for Beginners

ISBN: 978-1-7377542-8-2
contact info
stringsandivory@yahoo.com

I0146452

Scan QR Code

Amazon	Draft2Digital
Prints & eBooks	eBooks

Thank you so much for purchasing this book.
Strings & Ivory is designed to inspire
musicians, song writers, teachers and
students and is a one-stop,
comprehensive resource for musicians
who are looking for inspiration.

Jeffrey Carl

Table of Contents

Preface and Acknowledgements

Preface

As any musician knows, no matter what mood you're in, music is always there for you when you need it. It relates to your good moods, and your bad moods, your highs and your lows. It can inspire a person's budding creativity or sooth a troubled soul.

These are the things that have driven my passion to create this book. The goal of this project was to create a tool that is user friendly, easy to follow, and packed with information. My hope is that Strings & Ivory will inspire you to create beautiful music.

Acknowledgements

Special thanks to the following wonderful people whose input and constructive criticism made this book possible: Ashley Coey for her kind advice with the design elements, and S. Alise Bick for helping me to edit my final draft.

Understanding Chord Symbols

Chord Abbreviations

M	=	Major	m/M	=	minor/Major
Aug	=	Augmented	sus	=	suspended
m	=	minor	Dom	=	Dominant
dim	=	diminished			

Understanding Chord Symbols

There are three parts to the chord symbol.

	1. Abbreviation	2. Explicitly names degrees	3. Distinctive degrees
ex.	m	7	♭5

Put those examples together (m7♭5) and you have a minor 7th flat 5 chord.
Another example is M7♯5: Major 7th sharp 5
Here are a couple of exceptions:
1. Triads don't have explicitly named degrees in their symbol.

I	III+	vi	vii°
Uppercase Roman numeral is Major Chord	Plus symbol Roman numeral is Augmented Chord	Lowercase Roman numeral is Minor Chord	Degree symbol Roman numeral is Diminished Chord

Music Theory Terms

1. Tonal Music - Music that uses keys, chords & scales.
2. Note - A notation representing the pitch and duration of a musical sound.
3. Enharmonic - Notes of the same pitch that have different names.
4. Interval - The distance between two tones.
5. Chord - Three or more tones, sounded simultaneously.
6. Octave - The same tone, a pitch higher or a pitch lower.
7. Intervallic Formula - Formulas based on intervals.
8. Accidental - A sharp, flat, or natural not included in the given key.
9. Flat - A symbol which lowers the pitch of a note one-half step.
10. Double flat - A symbol which lowers the pitch of a note one whole step.
11. Triple Flat - A symbol which lowers the pitch of a note 1 1/2 steps.
12. Natural - A symbol which cancels a previous flat or sharp.
13. Sharp - A symbol which raises the pitch of a note one half step.
14. Double sharp - A symbol which raises the pitch of a note one whole step.
15. Harmony - Two or more tones sounded simultaneously.
16. Melody - In general, a succession of tones.
17. Key - A group of notes that relate to a single note called a tonic.
18. Parrallel Keys - Two different keys sharing the same tonic.
19. Relative Keys - Major and minor scales that have the same time signature.
20. Chord Progressions - A succession of musical chords.

Step Symbols and Accedental Symbols

Step Symbols

h   = half step
w   = whole step
wh   = 1 1/2 steps
ww   = 2 steps
wwh = 2 1/2 steps
www = 3 steps

Accedental Symbols

= Double Sharp
= Sharp
♮ = Natural
♭ = Flat
♭♭ = Double Flat
♭♭♭ = Triple Flat

Steps For Guitar

From any starting point on the guitar, if you move one fret over, it's a half step. If you move two frets, it's a whole step. If you move three frets, it's one and a half steps. If you move four frets, it's two whole steps. If you move five frets, it's two and a half steps. If you move 6 frets, it's three whole steps.

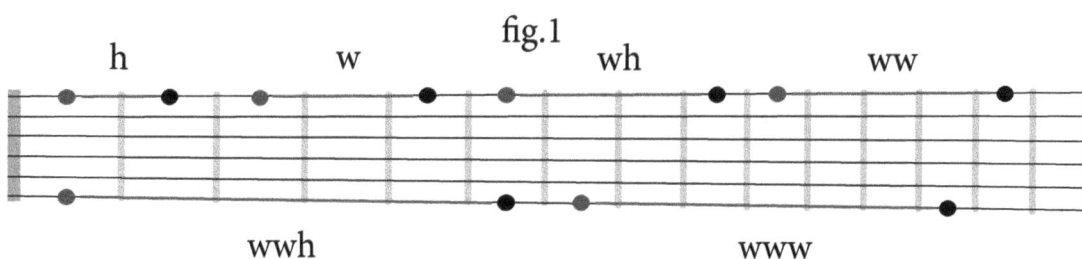

fig.1

Steps For Piano

From any starting point on the piano, if you span two piano keys, it's a half step. If you span three keys, it's a whole step. If you span four keys, its one and a half steps. If you span five keys, its two whole steps. If you span six keys, its two and a half steps. If you span seven keys, its three whole steps.

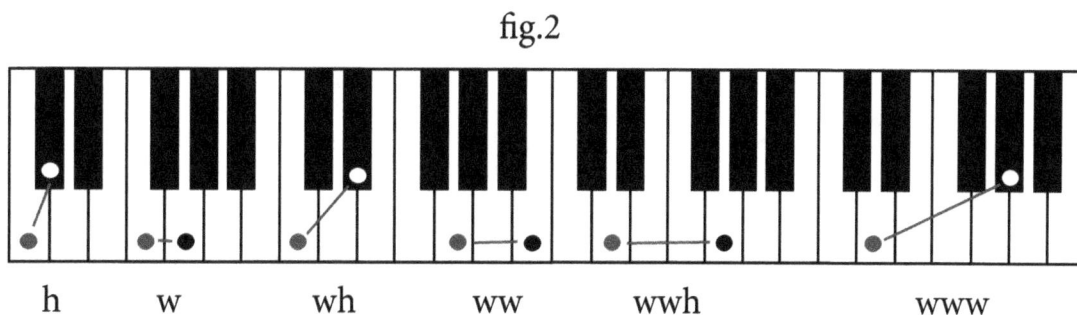

fig.2

Circle Of 5ths

To move in an interval of a perfect 5th, you must go clockwise. For example, a G is a perfect 5th interval from C, and a D is a perfect 5th interval from G. When going counter clockwise, you are moving in an interval of a perfect 4th. For example, F is a perfect 4th interval from C, and a B♭ is a perfect 4th interval from F. A perfect 4th interval and a perfect 5th interval are inversions of each other.

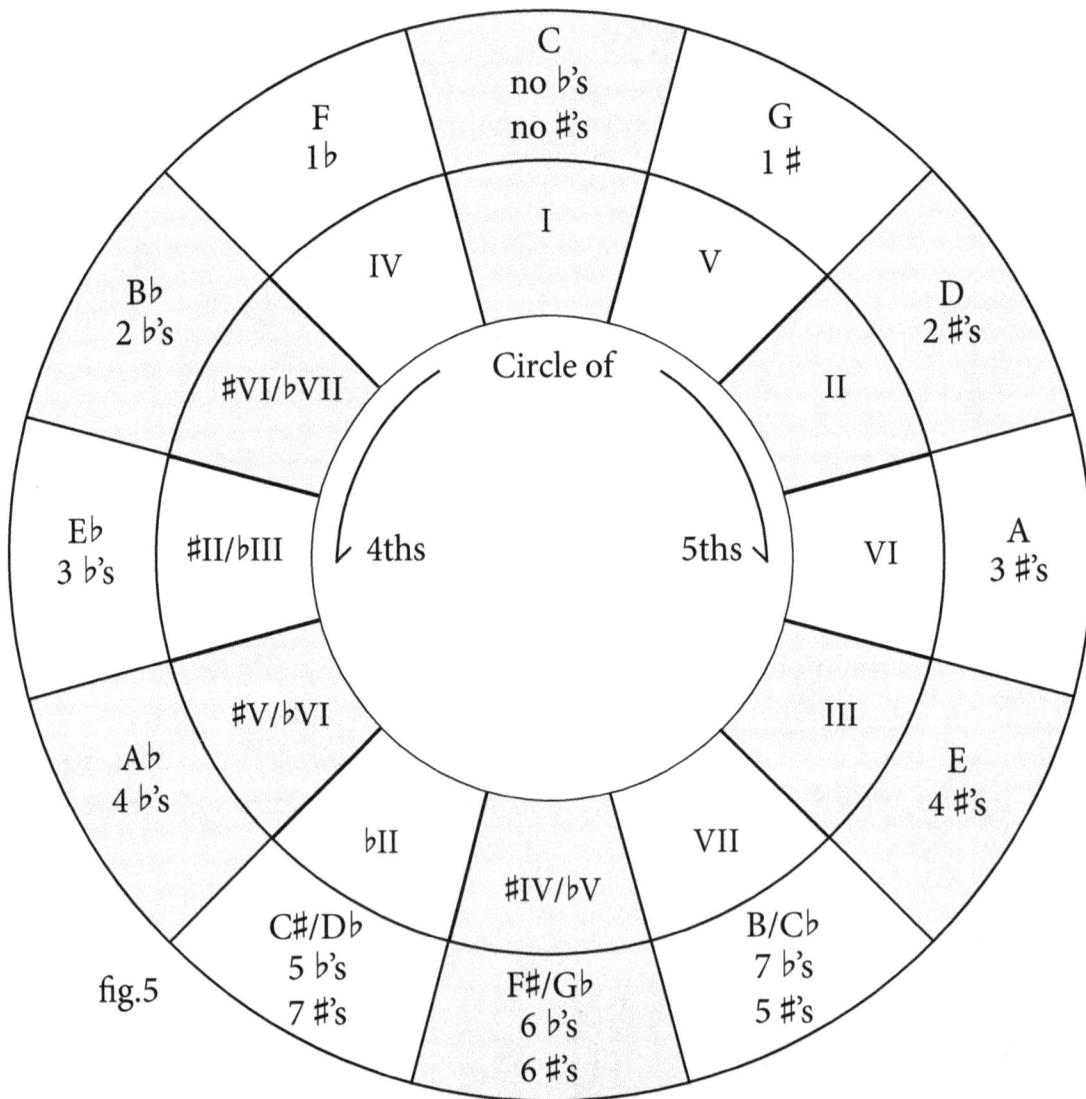

fig.5

Guitar Chords

Note Placement

The frets without notes can be either a flat note or a sharp note. For example the note between C & D can be either a C sharp or a D flat. Memorize all of the notes in the fretboard diagram below and it will be easy to know where all the sharp and flat notes are too. It will make it easy when trying to figure out where to play chords and scales.

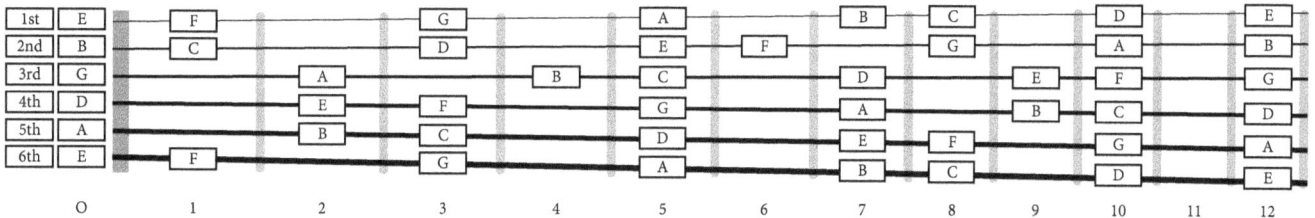

1st	E		F			G		A		B	C		D	E
2nd	B		C		D		E		F		G		A	B
3rd	G			A		B	C			D		E	F	G
4th	D		E		F		G		A		B	C		D
5th	A		B		C		D		E	F			G	A
6th	E		F		G		A		B	C			D	E

O 1 2 3 4 5 6 7 8 9 10 11 12

Understanding Chord Diagrams

Chords can be moved up and down the neck of the guitar. By doing this it does not change the type of chord it is, but only changes the notes that make up that chord. The targets in the chord diagrams are the root notes of the chord. Below we have one chord diagram of a Major Triad. On the fretboard diagram below we have the Major Triad chord in two different places. On the left side the target note is C making it a C Major Triad chord. On the right side the target note is G making it a G Major Triad chord.

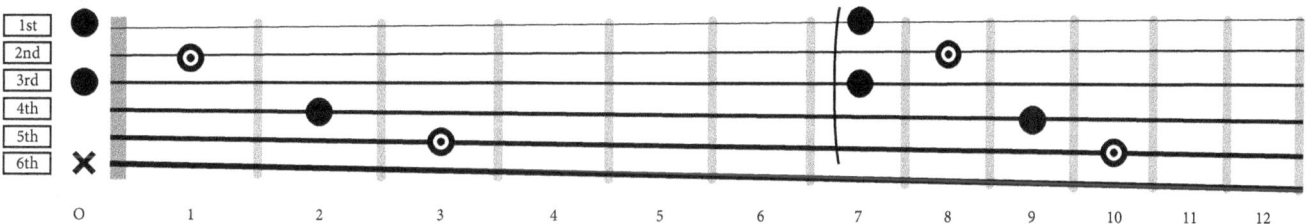

| 1st | 2nd | 3rd | 4th | 5th | 6th |

O 1 2 3 4 5 6 7 8 9 10 11 12

Major Triad

× ● ●

1 3 5 1 3

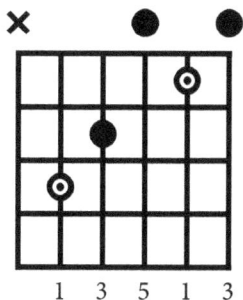

Chord Formula

When sliding a chord shape up the neck out of the open position you may need to bar the fretboard with your first finger to form the chord.

5

Major Triad (M)

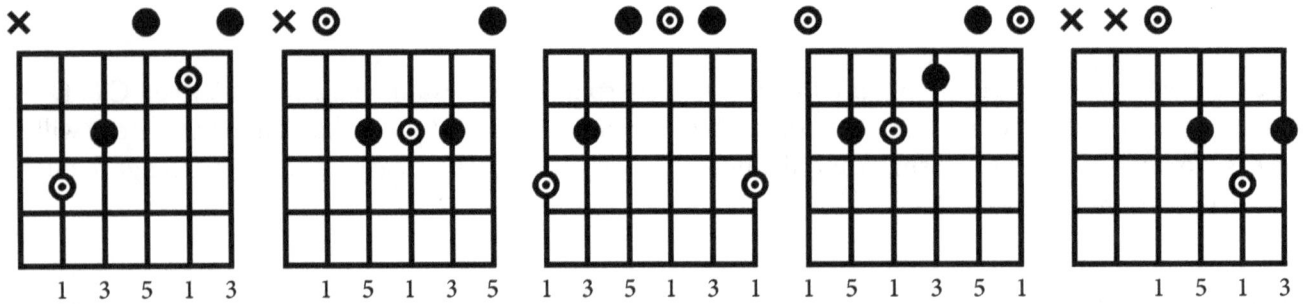

| 1 3 5 1 3 | 1 5 1 3 5 | 1 3 5 1 3 1 | 1 5 1 3 5 1 | 1 5 1 3 |

Augmented Triad (Aug)

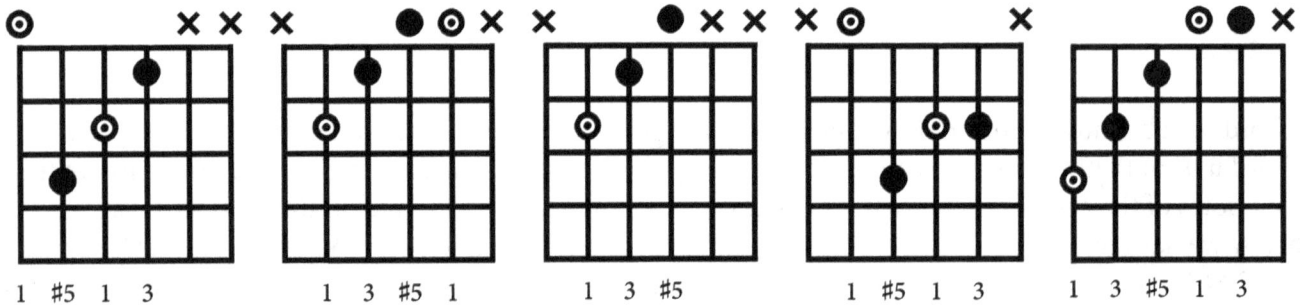

| 1 #5 1 3 | 1 3 #5 1 | 1 3 #5 | 1 #5 1 3 | 1 3 #5 1 3 |

Major add 9 (Madd9)

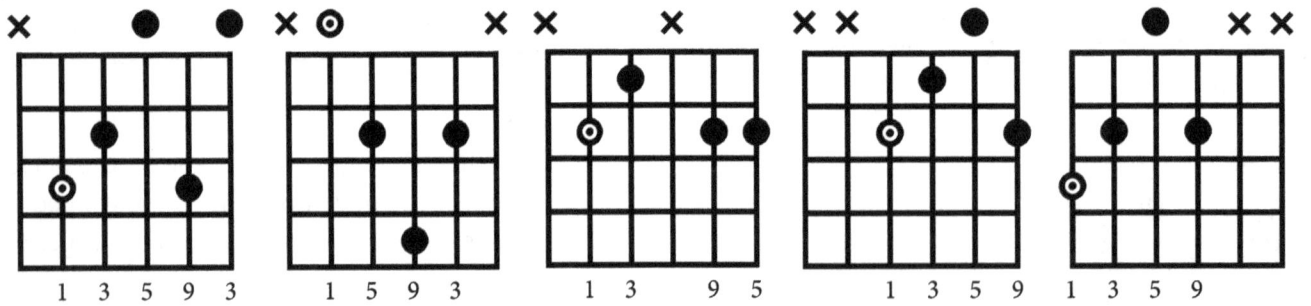

| 1 3 5 9 3 | 1 5 9 3 | 1 3 9 5 | 1 3 5 9 | 1 3 5 9 |

Major add 11 (Madd11)

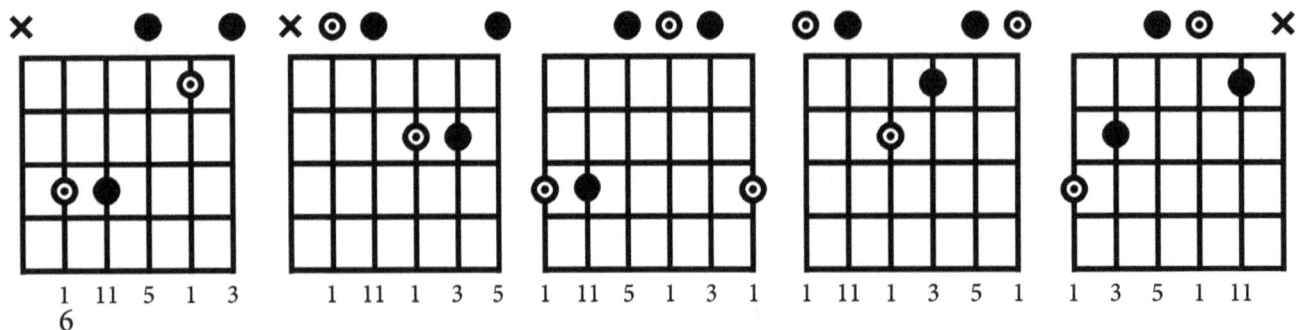

| 1 11 5 1 3 | 1 11 1 3 5 | 1 11 5 1 3 1 | 1 11 1 3 5 1 | 1 3 5 1 11 |

Major 6th (M6)

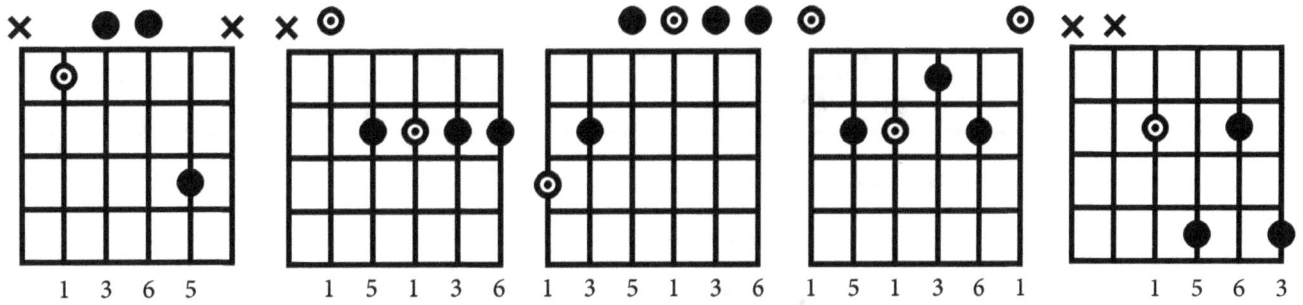

Major 7th (M7)

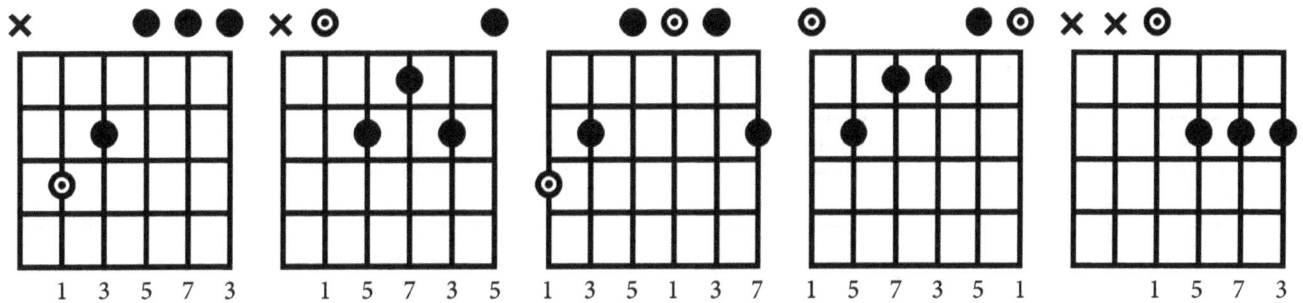

Major 7 #5 (M7#5)

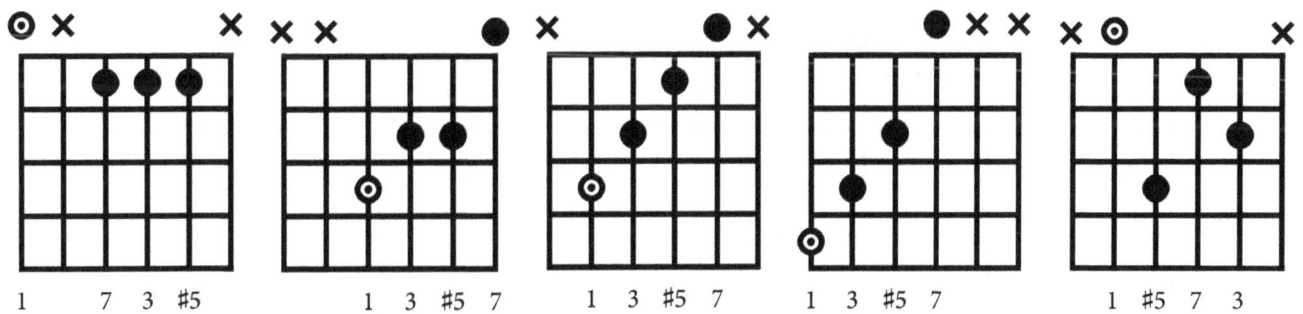

Minor Triad (m)

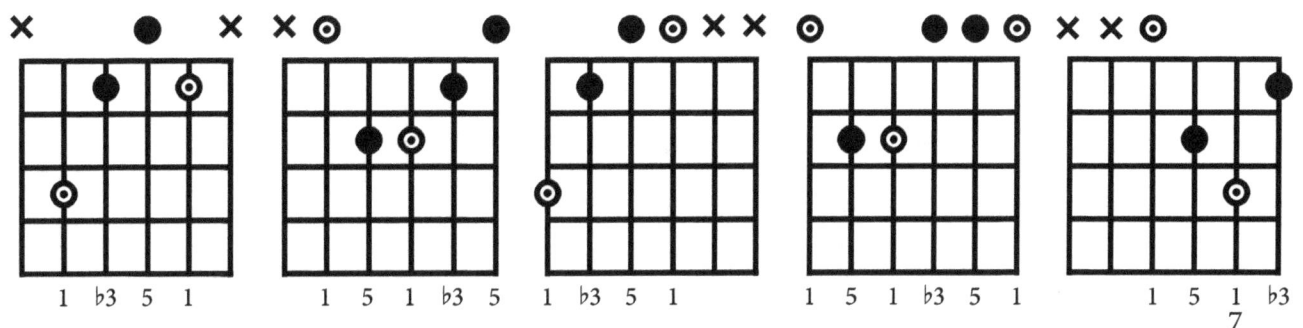

Diminished Triad (dim)

1 b3 b5 1   1 b3 b5 1   1 b5 1 b3   1 b5 1 b3   1 b3 b5

Minor add 9 (madd9)

1 b3 5 9   1 b3   9 5   1 b3 5 9   1 b3 5 9

Minor add 11 (madd11)

1 11 1 b3 5   1 11 1 b3 5 1

Minor 6th (m6)

1 b3 6   5   1 5 1 b3 6   1 5 6 b3   1 5 1 b3 6 1

8

Minor 7th (m7)

| 1 5 b7 b3 | 1 5 b7 b3 5 | 1 5 b7 b3 | 1 5 b7 b3 5 1 | 1 5 b7 b3 |

Minor 7 ♭5 (m7♭5) aka Half Diminished

| 1 b5 b7 b3 | 1 b5 b7 b3 | 1 b5 b7 b3 | | |

Diminished 7th (dim7)

| 1 b5 bb7 b3 | 1 b5 b3 bb7 | 1 b5 bb7 b3 | | |

Minor/Major 7th (m/M7)

| 1 5 7 b3 | 1 5 7 b3 5 | 1 5 7 b3 | 1 5 7 b3 5 1 | 1 5 7 b3 |

9

Dominant 7th (7 or Dom7)

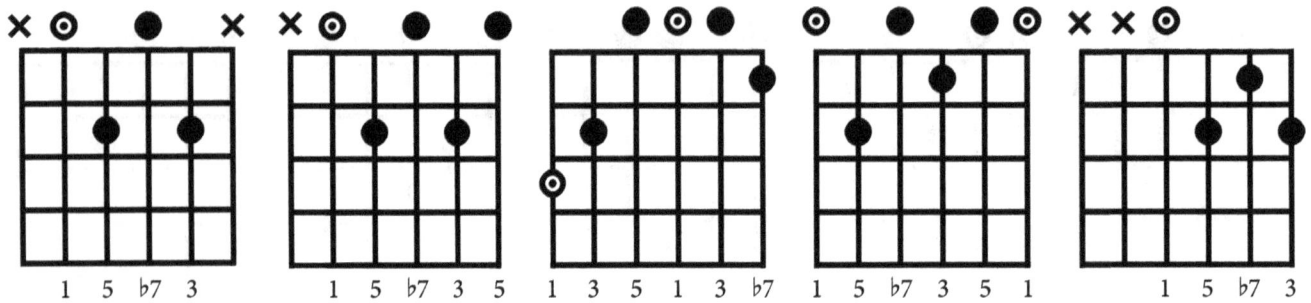

1 5 b7 3   1 5 b7 3 5   1 3 5 1 3 b7   1 5 b7 3 5 1   1 5 b7 3

Dominant 7 b5 (7b5 or Dom7b5)

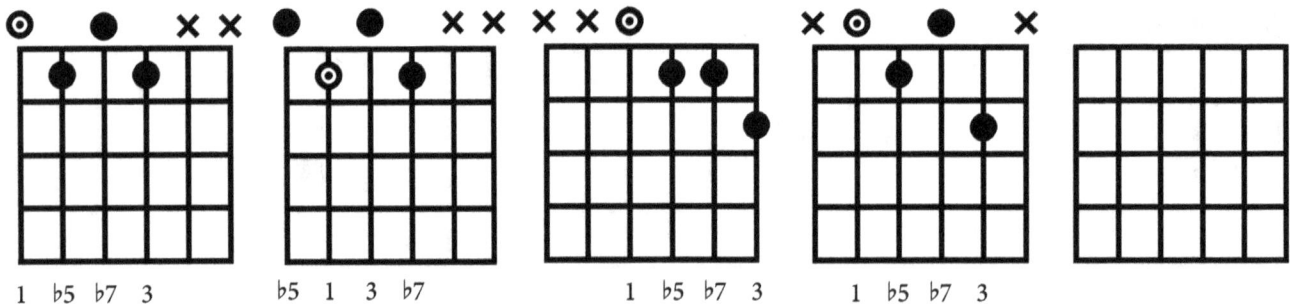

1 b5 b7 3   b5 1 3 b7   1 b5 b7 3   1 b5 b7 3

Augmented 7th (Aug7)

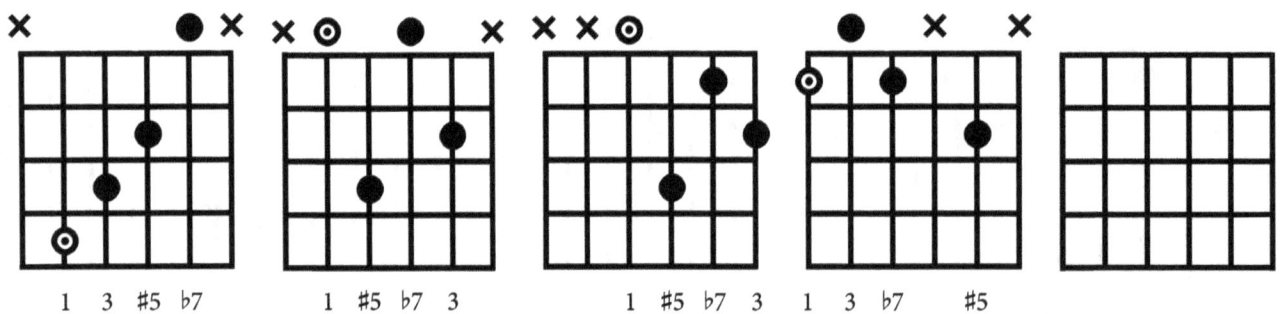

1 3 #5 b7   1 #5 b7 3   1 #5 b7 3   1 3 b7 #5

Suspended 2nd (sus2)

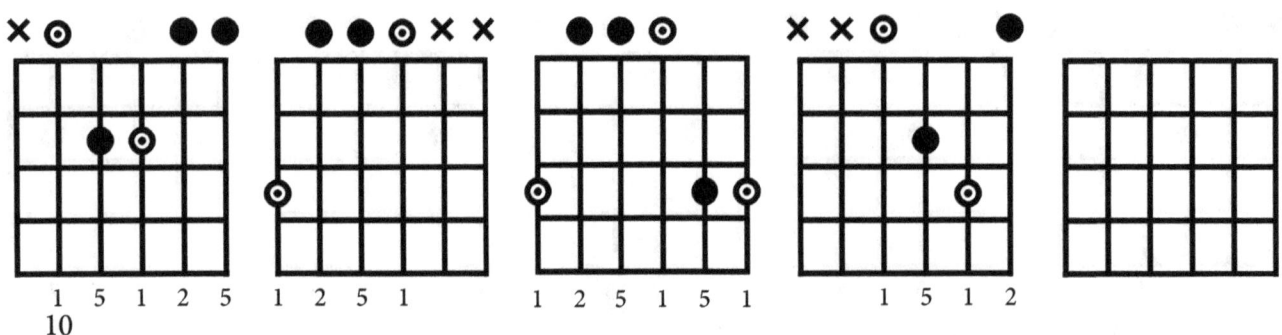

1 5 1 2 5   1 2 5 1   1 2 5 1 5 1   1 5 1 2

Suspended 4th (sus4)

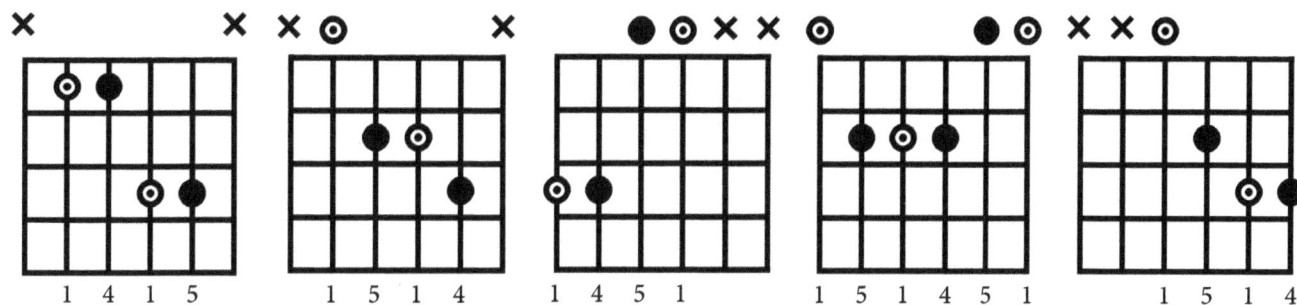

1 4 1 5   1 5 1 4   1 4 5 1   1 5 1 4 5 1   1 5 1 4

Major 7th Suspended 2nd (M7sus2)

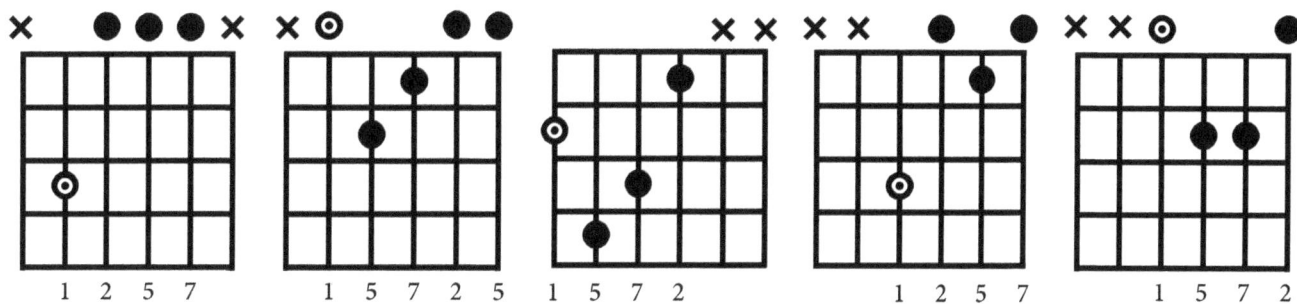

1 2 5 7   1 5 7 2 5   1 5 7 2   1 2 5 7   1 5 7 2

Major 7th Suspended 4th (M7sus4)

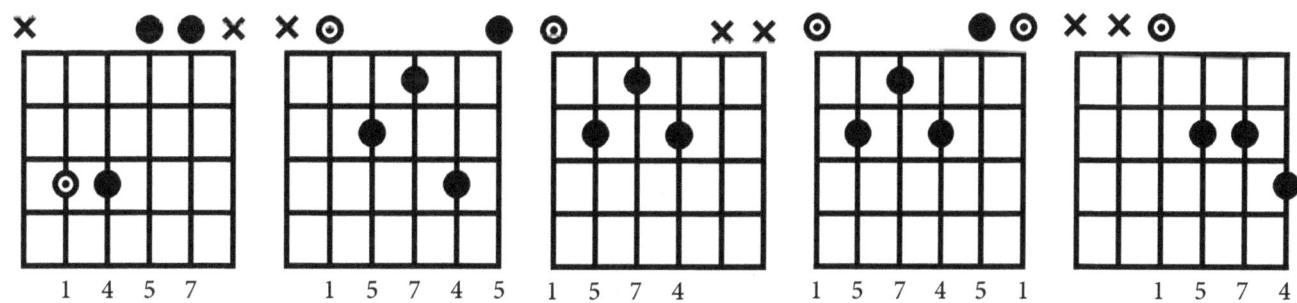

1 4 5 7   1 5 7 4 5   1 5 7 4   1 5 7 4 5 1   1 5 7 4

Dominant 7th Suspended 2nd (7sus2)

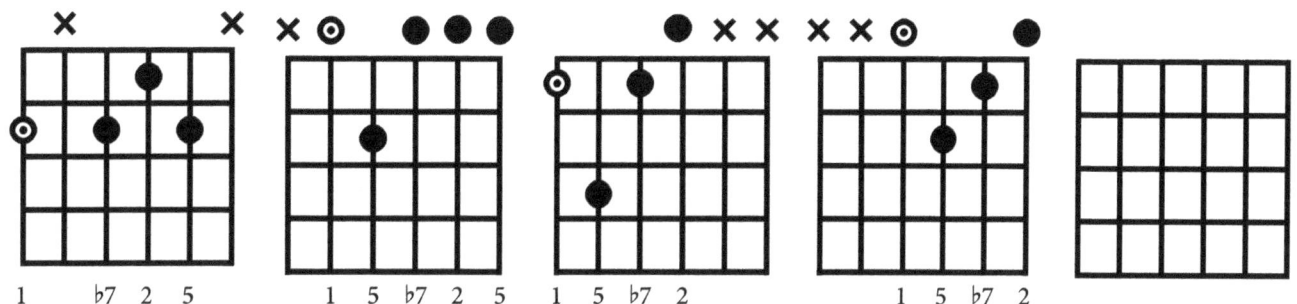

1 b7 2 5   1 5 b7 2 5   1 5 b7 2   1 5 b7 2

11

Dominant 7th Suspended 4th (7sus4)

Piano Chords

Major Triad

(M)

Augmented Triad

(Aug)

 C

 C#/Db

 D

 D#/Eb

 E

 F

 F#/Gb

 G

 G#/Ab

 A

 A#/Bb

 B

Major add 9
(Madd9)

Major add 11
(Madd11)

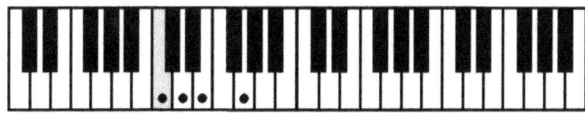 C

 C#/D♭

 D

 D#/E♭

 E

 F

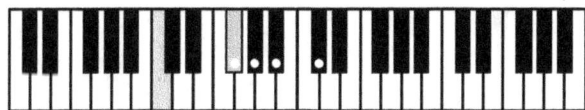 F#/G♭

 G

 G#/A♭

 A

 A#/B♭

 B

15

Major 6th

(M6)

Major 7th

(M7)

 C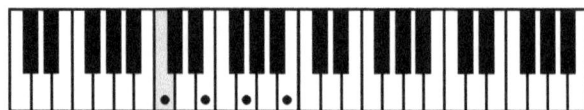

 C#/Db

 D

 D#/Eb

 E

 F

 F#/Gb

 G

 G#/Ab

 A

 A#/Bb

 B

Major 7 ♯ 5

(M7♯5)

Minor Triad

(m)

 C

 C♯/D♭

 D

 D♯/E♭

 E

 F

 F♯/G♭

 G

 G♯/A♭

 A

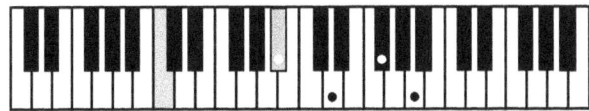 A♯/B♭

 B

17

Diminished Triad
(dim)

Minor add 9
(madd9)

 C

 C#/Db

 D

 D#/Eb

 E

 F

 F#/Gb

 G

 G#/Ab

 A

 A#/Bb

 B

Minor add 11   Minor 6th

(madd11)   (m6)

  C

  C#/Db

  D

  D#/Eb

  E

  F

  F#/Gb

  G

  G#/Ab

  A

  A#/Bb

  B

Minor 7th
(m7)

Minor 7 ♭5
(m7♭5)

 C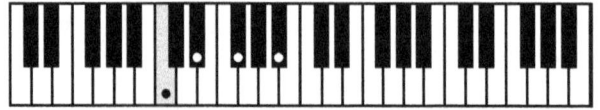

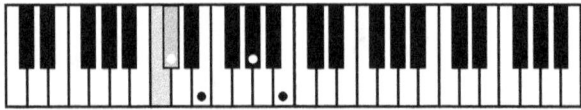 C#/D♭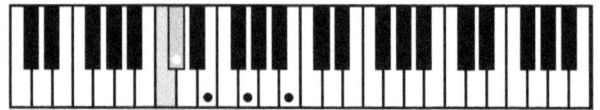

 D

 D#/E♭

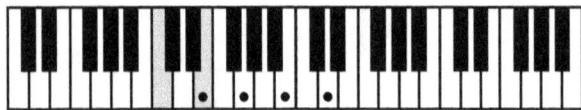 E

 F

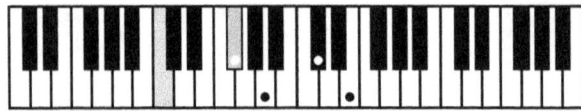 F#/G♭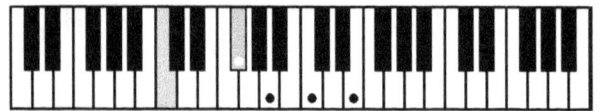

 G

 G#/A♭

 A

 A#/B♭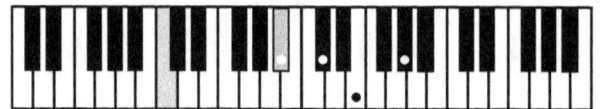

 B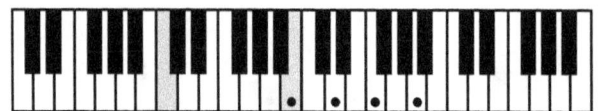

Diminished 7th
(dim7)

Minor/Major 7th
(m/M7)

  C

  C#/Db

  D

  D#/Eb

  E

  F

  F#/Gb

  G

  G#/Ab

  A

  A#/Bb

  B

Dominant 7th
(7 or Dom7)

Dominant 7 ♭5
(7♭5 or Dom7♭5)

	C	
	C#/D♭	
	D	
	D#/E♭	
	E	
	F	
	F#/G♭	
	G	
	G#/A♭	
	A	
	A#/B♭	
	B	

22

Augmented 7th
(Aug7)

Suspended 2nd
(sus2)

 C

 C#/D♭

 D

 D#/E♭

 E

 F

 F#/G♭

 G

 G#/A♭

 A

 A#/B♭

 B

23

Suspended 4th
(sus4)

Major 7th Sus 2nd
(M7sus2)

 C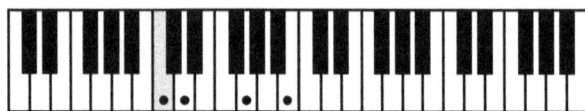

 C#/D♭

 D

 D#/E♭

 E

 F

 F#/G♭

 G

 G#/A♭

 A

 A#/B♭

 B

Major 7th Sus 4th
(M7sus4)

Dominant 7th Sus 2nd
(7sus2)

 C

 C#/Db

 D

 D#/Eb

 E

 F

 F#/Gb

 G

 G#/Ab

 A

 A#/Bb

 B

Dominant 7th Sus 4th

(7sus4)

 C

 C#/Db

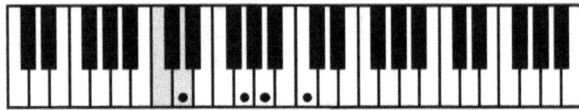 D

 D#/Eb

 E

 F

 F#/Gb

 G

 G#/Ab

 A

 A#/Bb

 B

Chord Spellings

Chord Spellings

Name	Abbreviation
Major	M

Chord Spellings

C = C,E,G
C# = C#,E#,G#
Db = Db,F,Ab
D = D,F#,A
D# = D#,F##,A#
Eb = Eb,G,Bb
E = E,G#,B
F = F,A,C

F# = F#,A#,C#
Gb = Gb,Bb,Db
G = G,B,D
G# = G#,B#,D#
Ab = Ab,C,Eb
A = A,C#,E
A# = A#,C##,E#
Bb = Bb,D,F
B = B,D#,F#

Name	Abbreviation
Augmented	Aug

Chord Spellings

C = C,E,G#
C# = C#,E#,G##
Db = Db,F,A
D = D,F#,A#
D# = D#,F##,A##
Eb = Eb,G,B
E = E,G#,B#
F = F,A,C#

F# = F#,A#,C##
Gb = Gb,Bb,D
G = G,B,D#
G# = G#,B#,D##
Ab = Ab,C,E
A = A,C#,E#
A# = A#,C##,E##
Bb = Bb,D,F#
B = B,D#,F##

Name	Abbreviation
Major Add 9	Madd9

Chord Spellings

C = C,E,G,D
C# = C#,E#,G#,D#
Db = Db,F,Ab,Eb
D = D,F#,A,E
D# = D#,F##,A#,E#
Eb = Eb,G,Bb,F
E = E,G#,B,F#
F = F,A,C,G

F# = F#,A#,C#,G#
Gb = Gb,Bb,Db,Ab
G = G,B,D,A
G# = G#,B#,D#,A#
Ab = Ab,C,Eb,Bb
A = A,C#,E,B
A# = A#,C##,E#,B#
Bb = Bb,D,F,C
B = B,D#,F#,C#

Chord Spellings

Name	Abbreviation
Major Add 11	Madd11

Chord Spellings

C = C,E,G,F   F# = F#,A#,C#,B
C# = C#,E#,G#,F#   Gb= Gb,Bb,Db,Cb
Db= Db,F,Ab,Gb   G = G,B,D,C
D = D,F#,A,G   G#= G#,B#,D#,C#
D#= D#,F##,A#,G#   Ab= Ab,C,Eb,Db
Eb= Eb,G,Bb,Ab   A = A,C#,E,D
E = E,G#,B,A   A# = A#,C##,E#,D#
F = F,A,C,Bb   Bb = Bb,D,F,Eb
    B = B,D#,F#,E

Name	Abbreviation
Major 6th	M6

Chord Spellings

C = C,E,G,A   F# = F#,A#,C#,D#
C# = C#,E#,G#,A#   Gb= Gb,Bb,Db,Eb
Db= Db,F,Ab,Bb   G = G,B,D,E
D = D,F#,A,B   G#= G#,B#,D#,E#
D#= D#,F##,A#,B#   Ab= Ab,C,Eb,F
Eb= Eb,G,Bb,C   A = Λ,C#,E,F#
E = E,G#,B,C#   A# = A#,C##,E#,F##
F = F,A,C,D   Bb = Bb,D,F,G
    B = B,D#,F#,G#

Name	Abbreviation
Major 7th	M7

Chord Spellings

C = C,E,G,B   F# = F#,A#,C#,E#
C# = C#,E#,G#,B#   Gb= Gb,Bb,Db,F
Db= Db,F,Ab,C   G = G,B,D,F#
D = D,F#,A,C#   G#= G#,B#,D#,F##
D#= D#,F##,A#,C##   Ab= Ab,C,Eb,G
Eb= Eb,G,Bb,D   A = A,C#,E,G#
E = E,G#,B,D#   A# = A#,C##,E#,G##
F = F,A,C,E   Bb = Bb,D,F,A
    B = B,D#,F#,A#

Chord Spellings

Name	Abbreviation
Major 7th #5	M7#5

Chord Spellings

C = C,E,G#,B		F# = F#,A#,C##,E#
C# = C#,E#,G##,B#		Gb = Gb,Bb,D,F
Db = Db,F,A,C		G = G,B,D#,F#
D = D,F#,A#,C#		G# = G#,B#,D##,F##
D# = D#,F##,A##,C##		Ab = Ab,C,E,G
Eb = Eb,G,B,D		A = A,C#,E#,G#
E = E,G#,B#,D#		A# = A#,C##,E##,G##
F = F,A,C#,E		Bb = Bb,D,F#,A
		B = B,D#,F##,A#

Name	Abbreviation
Minor	m

Chord Spellings

C = C,Eb,G		F# = F#,A,C#
C# = C#,E,G#		Gb = Gb,Bbb,Db
Db = Db,Fb,Ab		G = G,Bb,D
D = D,F,A		G# = G#,B,D#
D# = D#,F#,A#		Ab = Ab,Cb,Eb
Eb = Eb,Gb,Bb		A = A,C,E
E = E,G,B		A# = A#,C#,E#
F = F,Ab,C		Bb = Bb,Db,F
		B = B,D,F#

Name	Abbreviation
Diminished	Dim

Chord Spellings

C = C,Eb,Gb		F# = F#,A,C
C# = C#,E,G		Gb = Gb,Bbb,Dbb
Db = Db,Fb,Abb		G = G,Bb,Db
D = D,F,Ab		G# = G#,B,D
D# = D#,F#,A		Ab = Ab,Cb,Ebb
Eb = Eb,Gb,Bbb		A = A,C,Eb
E = E,G,Bb		A# = A#,C#,E
F = F,Ab,Cb		Bb = Bb,Db,Fb
		B = B,D,F

Chord Spellings

Name	Abbreviation
Minor Add 9	madd9

Chord Spellings

C = C,Eb,G,D
C# = C#,E,G#,D#
Db = Db,Fb,Ab,Eb
D = D,F,A,E
D# = D#,F#,A#,E#
Eb = Eb,Gb,Bb,F
E = E,G,B,F#
F = F,Ab,C,G

F# = F#,A,C#,G#
Gb = Gb,Bbb,Db,Ab
G = G,Bb,D,A
G# = G#,B,D#,A#
Ab = Ab,Cb,Eb,Bb
A = A,C,E,B
A# = A#,C#,E#,B#
Bb = Bb,Db,F,C
B = B,D,F#,C#

Name	Abbreviation
Minor Add 11	madd11

Chord Spellings

C = C,Eb,G,F
C# = C#,E,G#,F#
Db = Db,Fb,Ab,Gb
D = D,F,A,G
D# = D#,F#,A#,G#
Eb = Eb,Gb,Bb,Ab
E = E,G,B,A
F = F,Ab,C,Bb

F# = F#,A,C#,B
Gb = Gb,Bbb,Db,Cb
G = G,Bb,D,C
G# = G#,B,D#,C#
Ab = Ab,Cb,Eb,Db
A = A,C,E,D
A# = A#,C#,E#,D#
Bb = Bb,Db,F,Eb
B = B,D,F#,E

Name	Abbreviation
Minor 6th	m6

Chord Spellings

C = C,Eb,G,A
C# = C#,E,G#,A#
Db = Db,Fb,Ab,Bb
D = D,F,A,B
D# = D#,F#,A#,B#
Eb = Eb,Gb,Bb,C
E = E,G,B,C#
F = F,Ab,C,D

F# = F#,A,C#,D#
Gb = Gb,Bbb,Db,Eb
G = G,Bb,D,E
G# = G#,B,D#,E#
Ab = Ab,Cb,Eb,F
A = A,C,E,F#
A# = A#,C#,E#,F##
Bb = Bb,Db,F,G
B = B,D,F#,G#

Chord Spellings

Name	Abbreviation
Minor 7th	m7

Chord Spellings

C = C,Eb,G,Bb

C# = C#,E,G#,B

Db= Db,Fb,Ab,Cb

D = D,F,A,C

D#= D#,F#,A#,C#

Eb = Eb,Gb,Bb,Db

E = E,G,B,D

F = F,Ab,C,Eb

F# = F#,A,C#,E

Gb= Gb,Bbb,Db,Fb

G = G,Bb,D,F

G#= G#,B,D#,F#

Ab = Ab,Cb,Eb,Gb

A = A,C,E,G

A#= A#,C#,E#,G#

Bb = Bb,Db,F,Ab

B = B,D,F#,A

Name	Abbreviation
Minor 7th b5	m7b5

Chord Spellings

C = C,Eb,Gb,Bb

C# = C#,E,G,B

Db= Db,Fb,Abb,Cb

D = D,F,Ab,C

D#= D#,F#,A,C#

Eb = Eb,Gb,Bbb,Db

E = E,G,Bb,D

F = F,Ab,Cb,Eb

F# = F#,A,C,E

Gb= Gb,Bbb,Dbb,Fb

G = G,Bb,Db,F

G#= G#,B,D,F#

Ab = Ab,Cb,Ebb,Gb

A = A,C,Eb,G

A#= A#,C#,E,G#

Bb = Bb,Db,Fb,Ab

B = B,D,F,A

Name	Abbreviation
Diminished 7th	dim7

Chord Spellings

C = C,Eb,Gb,Bbb

C# = C#,E,G,Bb

Db= Db,Fb,Abb,Cbb

D = D,F,Ab,Cb

D#= D#,F#,A,C

Eb = Eb,Gb,Bbb,Dbb

E = E,G,Bb,Db

F = F,Ab,Cb,Ebb

F# = F#,A,C,Eb

Gb= Gb,Bbb,Dbb,Fbb

G = G,Bb,Db,Fb

G#= G#,B,D,F

Ab = Ab,Cb,Ebb,Gbb

A = A,C,Eb,Gb

A#= A#,C#,E,G

Bb = Bb,Db,Fb,Abb

B = B,D,F,Ab

Chord Spellings

Name	Abbreviation
Minor/Major 7th	m/M7

Chord Spellings

C = C,Eb,G,B
C# = C#,E,G#,B#
Db= Db,Fb,Ab,C
D = D,F,A,C#
D#= D#,F#,A#,C##
Eb = Eb,Gb,Bb,D
E = E,G,B,D#
F = F,Ab,C,E

F# = F#,A,C#,E#
Gb= Gb,Bbb,Db,F
G = G,Bb,D,F#
G#= G#,B,D#,F##
Ab = Ab,Cb,Eb,G
A = A,C,E,G#
A#= A#,C#,E#,G##
Bb = Bb,Db,F,A
B = B,D,F#,A#

Name	Abbreviation
Dominant 7th	7

Chord Spellings

C = C,E,G,Bb
C# = C#,E#,G#,B
Db= Db,F,Ab,Cb
D = D,F#,A,C
D#= D#,F##,A#,C#
Eb = Eb,G,Bb,Db
E = E,G#,B,D
F = F,A,C,Eb

F# = F#,A#,C#,E
Gb= Gb,Bb,Db,Fb
G = G,B,D,F
G#= G#,B#,D#,F#
Ab = Ab,C,Eb,Gb
A = A,C#,E,G
A#= A#,C##,E#,G#
Bb = Bb,D,F,Ab
B = B,D#,F#,A

Name	Abbreviation
Dominant 7th b5	7b5

Chord Spellings

C = C,E,Gb,Bb
C# = C#,E#,G,B
Db= Db,F,Abb,Cb
D = D,F#,Ab,C
D#= D#,F##,A,C#
Eb = Eb,G,Bbb,Db
E = E,G#,Bb,D
F = F,A,Cb,Eb

F# = F#,A#,C,E
Gb= Gb,Bb,Dbb,Fb
G = G,B,Db,F
G#= G#,B#,D,F#
Ab = Ab,C,Ebb,Gb
A = A,C#,Eb,G
A#= A#,C##,E,G#
Bb = Bb,D,Fb,Ab
B = B,D#,F,A

Chord Spellings

Name	Abbreviation
Augmented 7th	Aug7

Chord Spellings

C	= C,E,G♯,B♭	F♯	= F♯,A♯,C♯♯,E
C♯	= C♯,E♯,G♯♯,B	G♭	= G♭,B♭,D,F♭
D♭	= D♭,F,A,C♭	G	= G,B,D♯,F
D	= D,F♯,A♯,C	G♯	= G♯,B♯,D♯♯,F♯
D♯	= D♯,F♯♯,A♯♯,C♯	A♭	= A♭,C,E,G♭
E♭	= E♭,G,B,D♭	A	= A,C♯,E♯,G
E	= E,G♯,B♯,D	A♯	= A♯,C♯♯,E♯♯,G♯
F	= F,A,C♯,E♭	B♭	= B♭,D,F♯,A♭
		B	= B,D♯,F♯♯,A

Name	Abbreviation
Suspended 2nd	sus2

Chord Spellings

C	= C,G,D	F♯	= F♯,C♯,G♯
C♯	= C♯,G♯,D♯	G♭	= G♭,D♭,A♭
D♭	= D♭,A♭,E♭	G	= G,D,A
D	= D,A,E,	G♯	= G♯,D♯,A♯
D♯	= D♯,A♯,E♯	A♭	= A♭,E♭,B♭
E♭	= E♭,B♭,F	A	= A,E,B
E	= E,B,F♯	A♯	= A♯,E♯,B♯
F	= F,C,G	B♭	= B♭,F,C
		B	= B,F♯,C♯

Name	Abbreviation
Suspended 4th	sus4

Chord Spellings

C	= C,G,F,	F♯	= F♯,C♯,B
C♯	= C♯,G♯,F♯	G♭	= G♭,D♭,C♭
D♭	= D♭,A♭,G♭	G	= G,D,C
D	= D,A,G	G♯	= G♯,D♯,C♯
D♯	= D♯,A♯,G♯	A♭	= A♭,E♭,D♭
E♭	= E♭,B♭,A♭	A	= A,E,D
E	= E,B,A	A♯	= A♯,E♯,D♯
F	= F,C,B♭	B♭	= B♭,F,E♭
		B	= B,F♯,E

Chord Spellings

Name	Abbreviation
Major 7th Suspended 2nd	M7sus2

Chord Spellings

C = C,G,B,D
C# = C#,G#,B#,D#
Db = Db,Ab,C,Eb
D = D,A,C#,E
D# = D#,A#,C##,E#
Eb = Eb,Bb,D,F
E = E,B,D#,F#
F = F,C,E,G

F# = F#,C#,E#,G#
Gb = Gb,Db,F,Ab
G = G,D,F#,A
G# = G#,D#,F##,A#
Ab = Ab,Eb,G,Bb
A = A,E,G#,B
A# = A#,E#,G##,B#
Bb = Bb,F,A,C
B = B,F#,A#,C#

Name	Abbreviation
Major 7th Suspended 4th	M7sus4

Chord Spellings

C = C,G,B,F,
C# = C#,G#,B#,F#
Db = Db,Ab,C,Gb
D = D,A,C#,G
D# = D#,A#,C##,G#
Eb = Eb,Bb,D,Ab
E = E,B,D#,A
F = F,C,E,Bb

F# = F#,C#,E#,B
Gb = Gb,Db,F,Cb
G = G,D,F#,C
G# = G#,D#,F##,C#
Ab = Ab,Eb,G,Db
A = A,E,G#,D
A# = A#,E#,G##,D#
Bb = Bb,F,A,Eb
B = B,F#,A#,E

Name	Abbreviation
Dominant 7th Suspended 2nd	7sus2

Chord Spellings

C = C,G,Bb,D
C# = C#,G#,B,D#
Db = Db,Ab,Cb,Eb
D = D,A,C,E
D# = D#,A#,C#,E#
Eb = Eb,Bb,Db,F
E = E,B,D,F#
F = F,C,Eb,G

F# = F#,C#,E,G#
Gb = Gb,Db,Fb,Ab
G = G,D,F,A
G# = G#,D#,F#,A#
Ab = Ab,Eb,Gb,Bb
A = A,E,G,B
A# = A#,E#,G#,B#
Bb = Bb,F,Ab,C
B = B,F#,A,C#

Chord Spellings

Name	Abbreviation
Dominant 7th Suspended 4th	7sus4

Chord Spellings

C = C,G,B♭,F,

C♯ = C♯,G♯,B,F♯

D♭= D♭,A♭,C♭,G♭

D = D,A,C,G

D♯= D♯,A♯,C♯,G♯

E♭= E♭,B♭,D♭,A♭

E = E,B,D,A

F = F,C,E♭,B♭

F♯ = F♯,C♯,E,B

G♭= G♭,D♭,F♭,C♭

G = G,D,F,C

G♯= G♯,D♯,F♯,C♯

A♭= A♭,E♭,G♭,D♭

A = A,E,G,D

A♯= A♯,E♯,G♯,D♯

B♭= B♭,F,A♭,E♭

B = B,F♯,A,E

Chord Progression Flow Charts

Each degree of a scale has a function. These functions are put into groups called chord families. Below is our example of the Major scale and its modes.

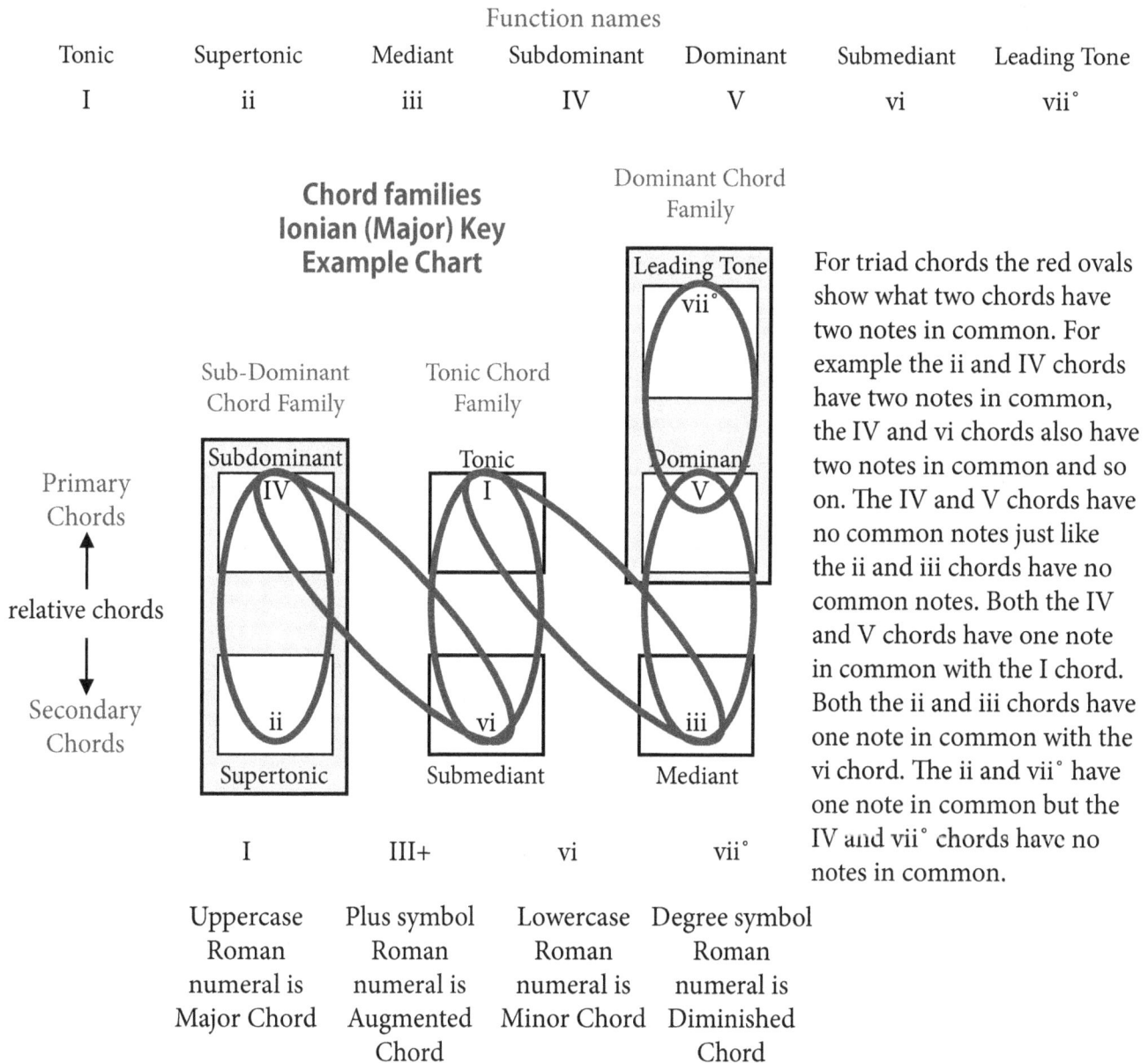

Function names

Tonic	Supertonic	Mediant	Subdominant	Dominant	Submediant	Leading Tone
I	ii	iii	IV	V	vi	vii°

**Chord families
Ionian (Major) Key
Example Chart**

Dominant Chord Family

Leading Tone
vii°

Sub-Dominant Chord Family

Tonic Chord Family

Primary Chords

Subdominant
IV

Tonic
I

Dominant
V

relative chords

Secondary Chords

ii
Supertonic

vi
Submediant

iii
Mediant

For triad chords the red ovals show what two chords have two notes in common. For example the ii and IV chords have two notes in common, the IV and vi chords also have two notes in common and so on. The IV and V chords have no common notes just like the ii and iii chords have no common notes. Both the IV and V chords have one note in common with the I chord. Both the ii and iii chords have one note in common with the vi chord. The ii and vii° have one note in common but the IV and vii° chords have no notes in common.

I	III+	vi	vii°
Uppercase Roman numeral is Major Chord	Plus symbol Roman numeral is Augmented Chord	Lowercase Roman numeral is Minor Chord	Degree symbol Roman numeral is Diminished Chord

Note:

1. Harmonized Chords are chords created from the scale.

2. Borrowed Chords are chords outside of the scale.

3. Below the Chord progression flow charts there is a list of Harmonized and borrowed chords. We can use one of these chords instead of the triad and 7th chords given in the flow chart.

4. When creating a chord progression do not use more than 1 or 2 borrowed chords because it will mess up the key you are trying to establish.

5. The Arrows show what chords you can go to next. The I-IV-V chord progression is the fountation of western music.

6. Chord progressions usually start with the "I" but they dont have to. Just experiment and have fun.

**Major Keys
Harmonic Progression
Diatonic Harmony**

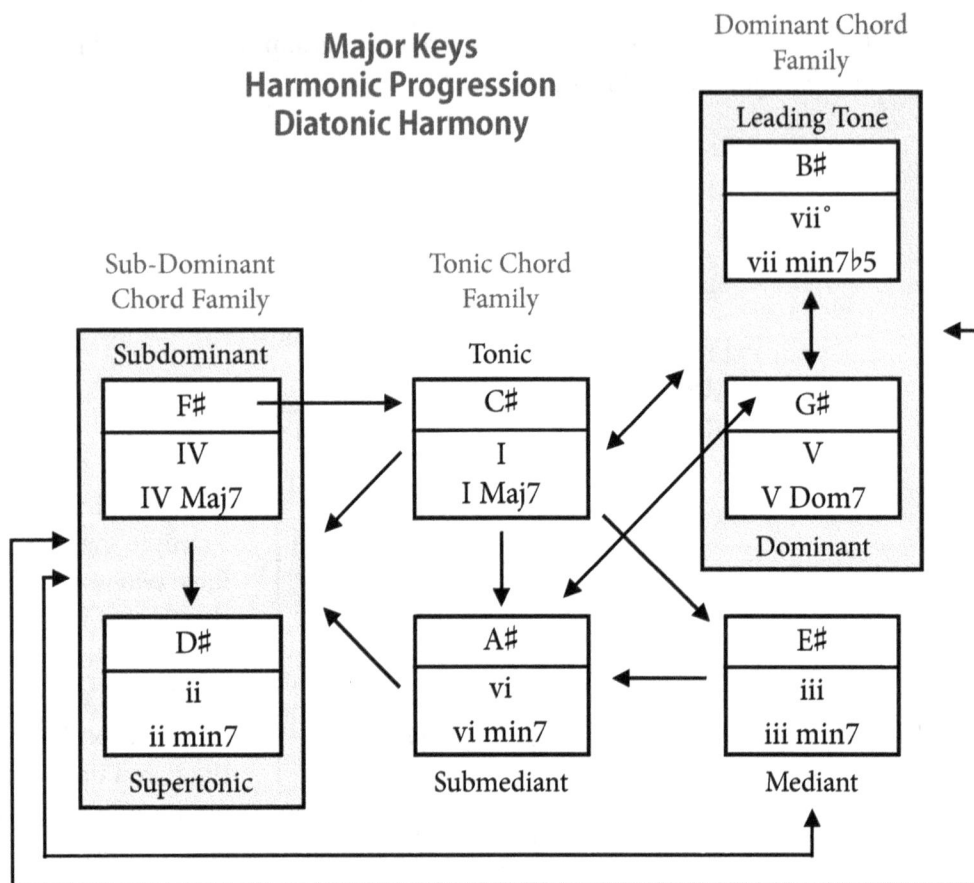

(D#) ii° / ii min7♭5 can go to the (B#) vii° / vii min7♭5

(E#) iii / iii min7 can go to the (B) ♭VII / ♭VII Maj7 / ♭VII Dom7 **and vise versa**

(A#) vi / vi min7 can go to the (B) ♭VII / ♭VII Maj7 / ♭VII Dom7 **and vise versa**

Degrees	C♯ Ionian	D♯ Dorian	E♯ Phrygian	F♯ Lydian
Harmonized Chords	M, Madd9, Madd11, M6, Sus2, Sus4, M7sus2, M7sus4, M7	m, madd9, madd11, m6, sus2, sus4, 7sus2, 7sus4, m7	m, madd11, sus4, 7sus4, m7	M, Madd9, M6, sus2, M7sus2, M7
Borrowed Chords	I Dom7	ii° ii min7♭5	iii° iii min7♭5	iv iv min/Maj7
Degrees	G♯ Mixolydian	A♯ Aeolian	B♯ Locrian	
Harmonized Chords	M, Madd9, Madd11, M6, sus2, sus4, 7sus2, 7sus4, 7	m, madd9, madd11, sus2, sus4, 7sus2, 7sus4, m7	dim, m7♭5	Chords built off of the Flat 7th degree are Sub-Tonic instead of Leading Tone.
Borrowed Chords	v v min7	A ♭VI+ A ♭VI Maj7#5	B ♭VII B ♭VII Maj7	B ♭VII Dom7 B♯ vii° 7

Chord Progression Chart in Key of C♯ Minor

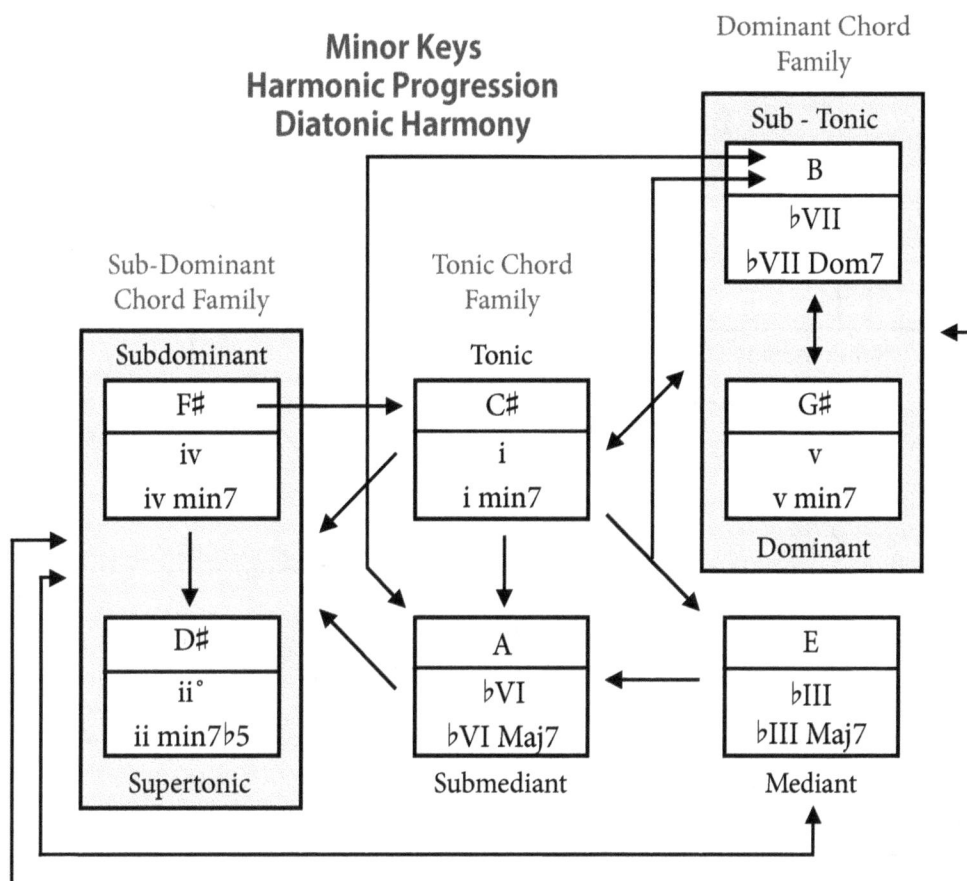

**Minor Keys
Harmonic Progression
Diatonic Harmony**

Dominant Chord
Family

Sub-Dominant
Chord Family

Tonic Chord
Family

Sub - Tonic

B
♭VII
♭VII Dom7

Subdominant

F♯
iv
iv min7

Tonic

C♯
i
i min7

G♯
v
v min7

Dominant

D♯
ii°
ii min7♭5

Supertonic

A
♭VI
♭VI Maj7

Submediant

E
♭III
♭III Maj7

Mediant

(D♯) ii° / ii min7♭5 can go to the (B♯) vii° / vii min7♭5

(A) ♭VI / ♭VI Maj7 can go to the (G♯) V / V Dom7 **and vise versa**

Degrees	C♯ Aeolian	D♯ Locrian	E Ionian	F♯ Dorian
Harmonized Chords	m, madd9, madd11, sus2, sus4, 7sus2, 7sus4, m7	dim, m7♭5	M, Madd9, Madd11, M6, Sus2, Sus4, M7sus2, M7sus4, M7	m, madd9, madd11, m6, sus2, sus4, 7sus2, 7sus4, m7
Borrowed Chords	i min/Maj7	ii ii min7	♭III+ ♭III Maj7♯5	IV IV Dom7

Degrees	G♯ Phrygian	A Lydian	B Mixolydian	
Harmonized Chords	m, madd11, sus4, 7sus4, m7	M, Madd9, M6, sus2, M7sus2, M7	M, Madd9, Madd11, M6, sus2, sus4, 7sus2, 7sus4, 7	Chords built off of the Natural 7th degree are Leading Tone instead of Sub-Tonic.
Borrowed Chords	V V Dom7	A♯ vi° A♯ vi min7♭5	B♯ vii° B♯ vii°7	B♯ vii min7♭5 B ♭VII Maj7

Chord Progression Chart in Key of F♯ Major

**Major Keys
Harmonic Progression
Diatonic Harmony**

Dominant Chord Family

Leading Tone

E♯
vii°
vii min7♭5

Sub-Dominant Chord Family

Subdominant

B
IV
IV Maj7

G♯
ii
ii min7

Supertonic

Tonic Chord Family

Tonic

F♯
I
I Maj7

D♯
vi
vi min7

Submediant

C♯
V
V Dom7

Dominant

A♯
iii
iii min7

Mediant

(G♯) ii° / ii min7♭5 can go to the (E♯) vii° / vii min7♭5

(A♯) iii / iii min7 can go to the (E) ♭VII / ♭VII Maj7 / ♭VII Dom7 **and vise versa**

(D♯) vi / vi min7 can go to the (E) ♭VII / ♭VII Maj7 / ♭VII Dom7 **and vise versa**

Degrees	F♯ Ionian	G♯ Dorian	A♯ Phrygian	B Lydian
Harmonized Chords	M, Madd9, Madd11, M6, Sus2, Sus4, M7sus2, M7sus4, M7	m, madd9, madd11, m6, sus2, sus4, 7sus2, 7sus4, m7	m, madd11, sus4, 7sus4, m7	M, Madd9, M6, sus2, M7sus2, M7
Borrowed Chords	I Dom7	ii° ii min7♭5	iii° iii min7♭5	iv iv min/Maj7
Degrees	C♯ Mixolydian	D♯ Aeolian	E♯ Locrian	
Harmonized Chords	M, Madd9, Madd11, M6, sus2, sus4, 7sus2, 7sus4, 7	m, madd9, madd11, sus2, sus4, 7sus2, 7sus4, m7	dim, m7♭5	Chords built off of the Flat 7th degree are Sub-Tonic instead of Leading Tone.
Borrowed Chords	v v min7	D ♭VI+ D ♭VI Maj7♯5	E ♭VII E ♭VII Maj7	E ♭VII Dom7 E♯ vii° 7

40

Chord Progression Chart in Key of F♯ Minor

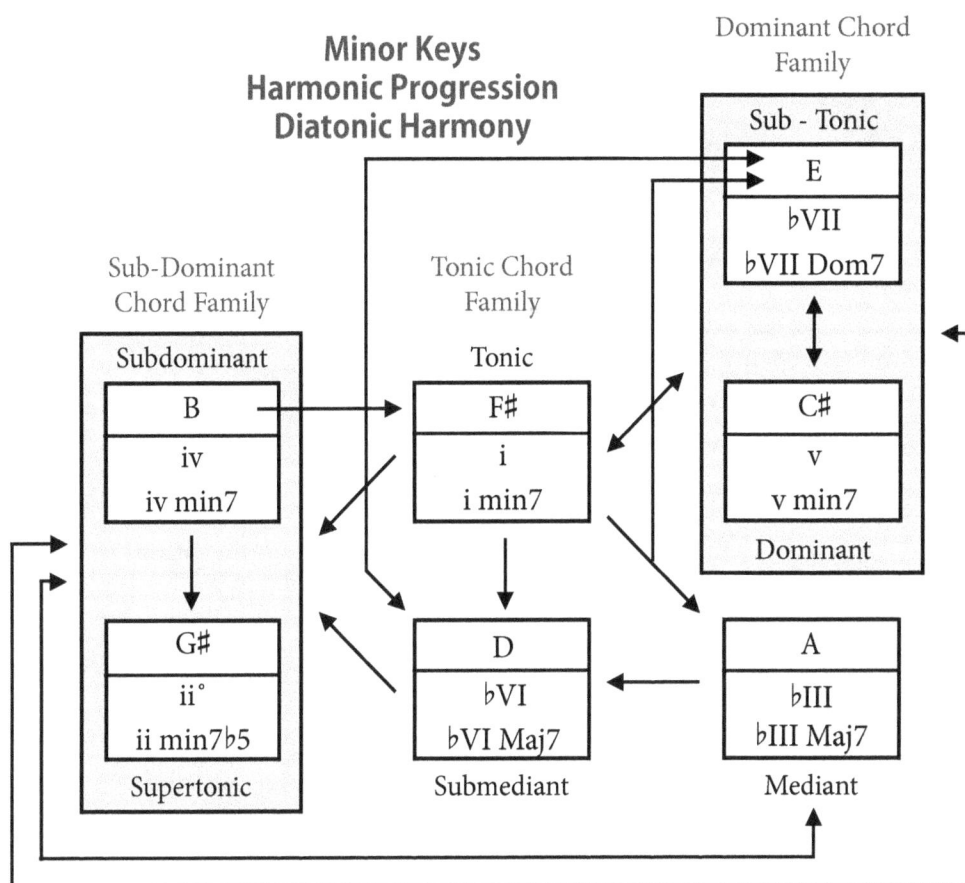

**Minor Keys
Harmonic Progression
Diatonic Harmony**

Dominant Chord Family

Sub - Tonic

E
♭VII
♭VII Dom7

Sub-Dominant Chord Family

Subdominant

B
iv
iv min7

Tonic Chord Family

Tonic

F♯
i
i min7

C♯
v
v min7

Dominant

G♯
ii°
ii min7♭5

Supertonic

D
♭VI
♭VI Maj7

Submediant

A
♭III
♭III Maj7

Mediant

(G♯) ii° / ii min7♭5 can go to the (E♯) vii° / vii min7♭5

(D) ♭VI / ♭VI Maj7 can go to the (C♯) V / V Dom7 **and vise versa**

Degrees	F♯ Aeolian	G♯ Locrian	A Ionian	B Dorian
Harmonized Chords	m, madd9, madd11, sus2, sus4, 7sus2, 7sus4, m7	dim, m7♭5	M, Madd9, Madd11, M6, Sus2, Sus4, M7sus2, M7sus4, M7	m, madd9, madd11, m6, sus2, sus4, 7sus2, 7sus4, m7
Borrowed Chords	i min/Maj7	ii ii min7	♭III+ ♭III Maj7♯5	IV IV Dom7

Degrees	C♯ Phrygian	D Lydian	E Mixolydian	
Harmonized Chords	m, madd11, sus4, 7sus4, m7	M, Madd9, M6, sus2, M7sus2, M7	M, Madd9, Madd11, M6, sus2, sus4, 7sus2, 7sus4, 7	Chords built off of the Natural 7th degree are Leading Tone instead of Sub-Tonic.
Borrowed Chords	V V Dom7	D♯ vi° D♯ vi min7♭5	E♯ vii° E♯ vii°7	E♯ vii min7♭5 E ♭VII Maj7

Chord Progression Chart in Key of B Major

Major Keys
Harmonic Progression
Diatonic Harmony

Dominant Chord Family

Sub-Dominant Chord Family

Tonic Chord Family

(C#) ii° / ii min7♭5 can go to the (A#) vii° / vii min7♭5

(D#) iii / iii min7 can go to the (A) ♭VII / ♭VII Maj7 / ♭VII Dom7 **and vise versa**

(G#) vi / vi min7 can go to the (A) ♭VII / ♭VII Maj7 / ♭VII Dom7 **and vise versa**

Degrees	B Ionian	C# Dorian	D# Phrygian	E Lydian
Harmonized Chords	M, Madd9, Madd11, M6, Sus2, Sus4, M7sus2, M7sus4, M7	m, madd9, madd11, m6, sus2, sus4, 7sus2, 7sus4, m7	m, madd11, sus4, 7sus4, m7	M, Madd9, M6, sus2, M7sus2, M7
Borrowed Chords	I Dom7	ii° ii min7♭5	iii° iii min7♭5	iv iv min/Maj7
Degrees	F# Mixolydian	G# Aeolian	A# Locrian	
Harmonized Chords	M, Madd9, Madd11, M6, sus2, sus4, 7sus2, 7sus4, 7	m, madd9, madd11, sus2, sus4, 7sus2, 7sus4, m7	dim, m7♭5	Chords built off of the Flat 7th degree are Sub-Tonic instead of Leading Tone.
Borrowed Chords	v v min7	G ♭VI+ G ♭VI Maj7#5	A ♭VII A ♭VII Maj7	A ♭VII Dom7 A# vii° 7

Chord Progression Chart in Key of B Minor

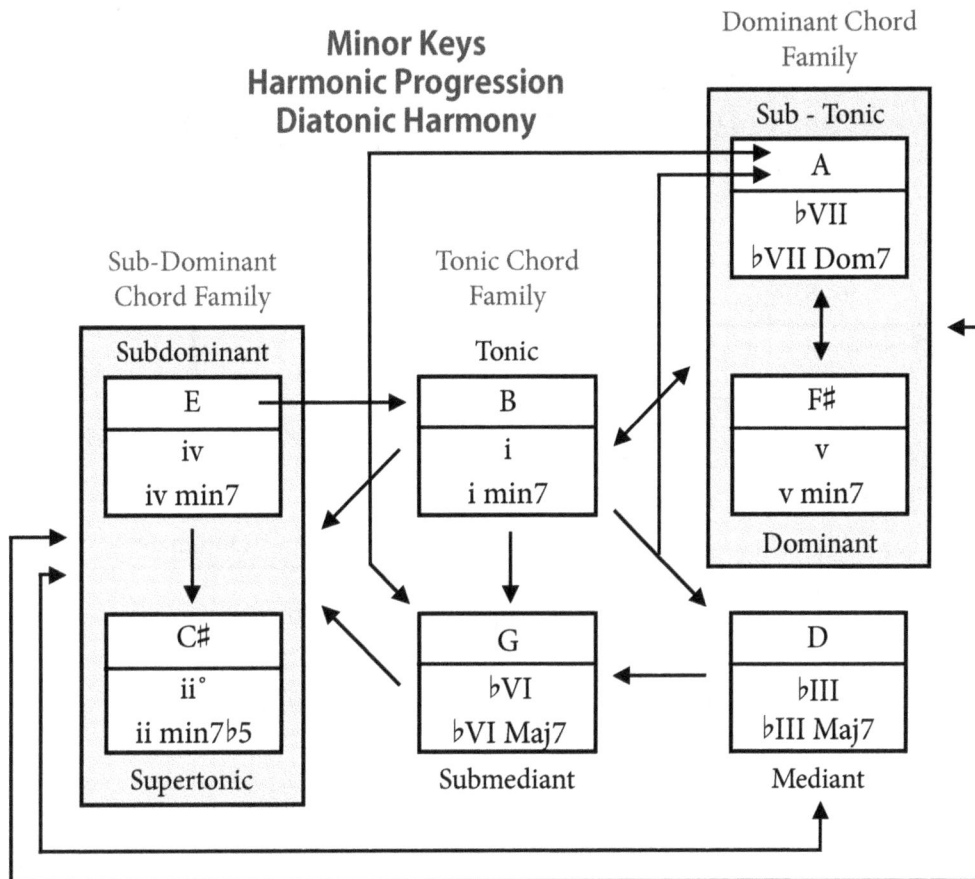

Minor Keys
Harmonic Progression
Diatonic Harmony

Dominant Chord Family

Sub-Dominant Chord Family

Tonic Chord Family

Sub - Tonic

| A |
| ♭VII |
| ♭VII Dom7 |

Subdominant

| E |
| iv |
| iv min7 |

Tonic

| B |
| i |
| i min7 |

| F# |
| v |
| v min7 |

Dominant

| C# |
| ii° |
| ii min7♭5 |

Supertonic

| G |
| ♭VI |
| ♭VI Maj7 |

Submediant

| D |
| ♭III |
| ♭III Maj7 |

Mediant

(C#) ii° / ii min7♭5 can go to the (A#) vii° / vii min7♭5

(G) ♭VI / ♭VI Maj7 can go to the (F#) V / V Dom7 **and vise versa**

Degrees	B Aeolian	C# Locrian	D Ionian	E Dorian
Harmonized Chords	m, madd9, madd11, sus2, sus4, 7sus2, 7sus4, m7	dim, m7♭5	M, Madd9, Madd11, M6, Sus2, Sus4, M7sus2, M7sus4, M7	m, madd9, madd11, m6, sus2, sus4, 7sus2, 7sus4, m7
Borrowed Chords	i min/Maj7	ii ii min7	♭III+ ♭III Maj7#5	IV IV Dom7

Degrees	F# Phrygian	G Lydian	A Mixolydian	
Harmonized Chords	m, madd11, sus4, 7sus4, m7	M, Madd9, M6, sus2, M7sus2, M7	M, Madd9, Madd11, M6, sus2, sus4, 7sus2, 7sus4, 7	Chords built off of the Natural 7th degree are Leading Tone instead of Sub-Tonic.
Borrowed Chords	V V Dom7	G# vi° G# vi min7♭5	A# vii° A# vii°7	A# vii min7♭5 A ♭VII Maj7

43

Chord Progression Chart in Key of E Major

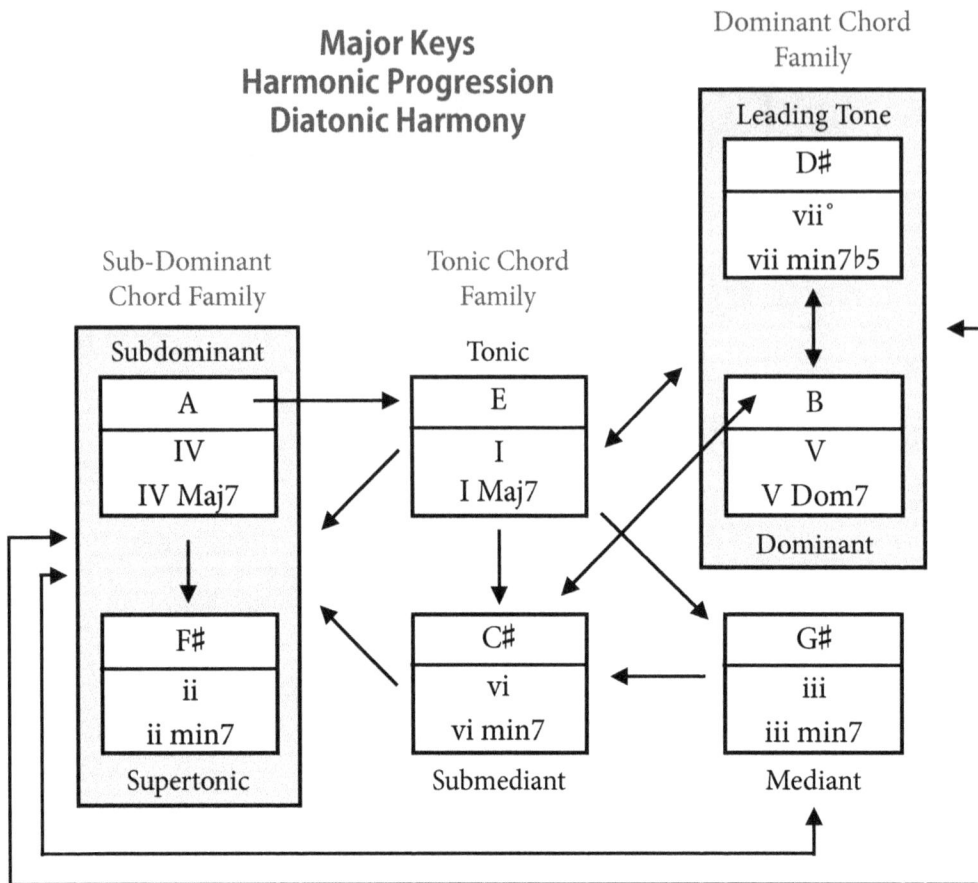

Major Keys
Harmonic Progression
Diatonic Harmony

Dominant Chord
Family

Leading Tone

D#
vii°
vii min7♭5

Sub-Dominant
Chord Family

Tonic Chord
Family

Subdominant

A
IV
IV Maj7

Tonic

E
I
I Maj7

B
V
V Dom7

Dominant

F#
ii
ii min7

Supertonic

C#
vi
vi min7

Submediant

G#
iii
iii min7

Mediant

(F#) ii° / ii min7♭5 can go to the (D#) vii° / vii min7♭5

(G#) iii / iii min7 can go to the (D) ♭VII / ♭VII Maj7 / ♭VII Dom7 **and vise versa**

(C#) vi / vi min7 can go to the (D) ♭VII / ♭VII Maj7 / ♭VII Dom7 **and vise versa**

Degrees	E Ionian	F# Dorian	G# Phrygian	A Lydian
Harmonized Chords	M, Madd9, Madd11, M6, Sus2, Sus4, M7sus2, M7sus4, M7	m, madd9, madd11, m6, sus2, sus4, 7sus2, 7sus4, m7	m, madd11, sus4, 7sus4, m7	M, Madd9, M6, sus2, M7sus2, M7
Borrowed Chords	I Dom7	ii° ii min7♭5	iii° iii min7♭5	iv iv min/Maj7

Degrees	B Mixolydian	C# Aeolian	D# Locrian	
Harmonized Chords	M, Madd9, Madd11, M6, sus2, sus4, 7sus2, 7sus4, 7	m, madd9, madd11, sus2, sus4, 7sus2, 7sus4, m7	dim, m7♭5	Chords built off of the Flat 7th degree are Sub-Tonic instead of Leading Tone.
Borrowed Chords	v v min7	C ♭VI+ C ♭VI Maj7#5	D ♭VII D ♭VII Maj7	D ♭VII Dom7 D# vii° 7

Chord Progression Chart in Key of E Minor

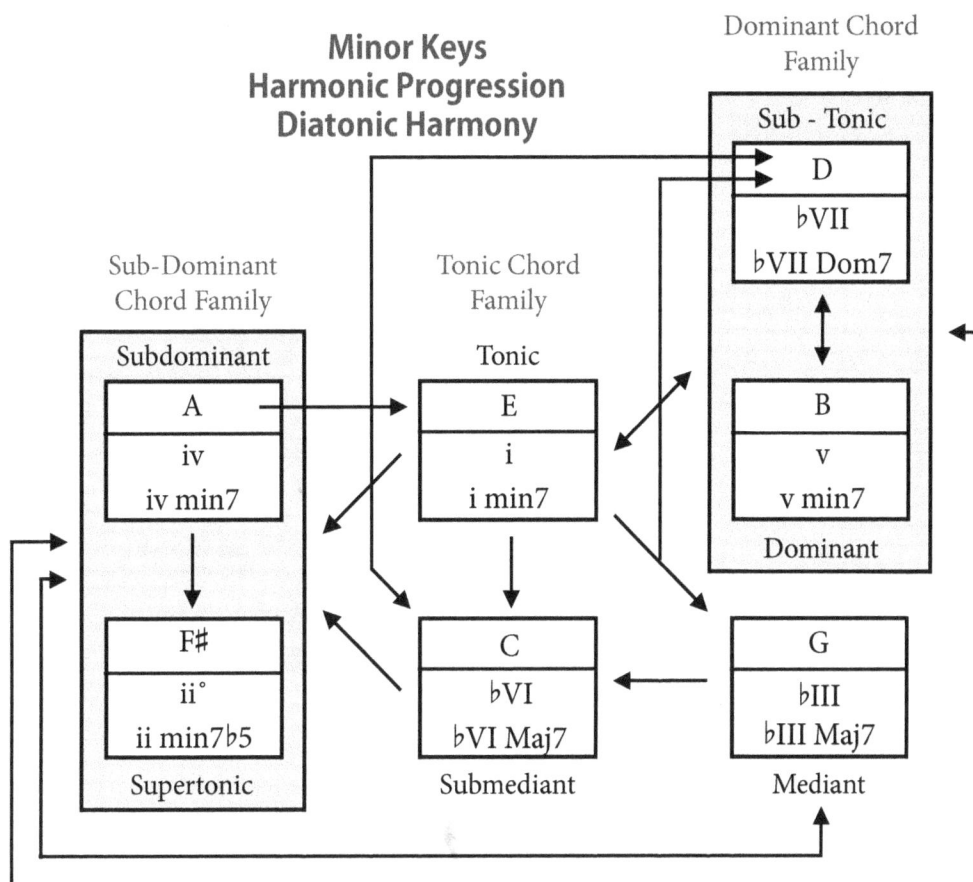

Minor Keys
Harmonic Progression
Diatonic Harmony

Dominant Chord Family

Sub-Dominant Chord Family

Tonic Chord Family

Sub - Tonic
D
♭VII
♭VII Dom7

Subdominant
A
iv
iv min7

Tonic
E
i
i min7

B
v
v min7

Dominant

F#
ii°
ii min7♭5

Supertonic

C
♭VI
♭VI Maj7

Submediant

G
♭III
♭III Maj7

Mediant

(F#) ii° / ii min7♭5 can go to the (D#) vii° / vii min7♭5

(C) ♭VI / ♭VI Maj7 can go to the (B) V / V Dom7 **and vise versa**

Degrees	E Aeolian	F# Locrian	G Ionian	A Dorian
Harmonized Chords	m, madd9, madd11, sus2, sus4, 7sus2, 7sus4, m7	dim, m7♭5	M, Madd9, Madd11, M6, Sus2, Sus4, M7sus2, M7sus4, M7	m, madd9, madd11, m6, sus2, sus4, 7sus2, 7sus4, m7
Borrowed Chords	i min/Maj7	ii ii min7	♭III+ ♭III Maj7#5	IV IV Dom7

Degrees	B Phrygian	C Lydian	D Mixolydian	
Harmonized Chords	m, madd11, sus4, 7sus4, m7	M, Madd9, M6, sus2, M7sus2, M7	M, Madd9, Madd11, M6, sus2, sus4, 7sus2, 7sus4, 7	Chords built off of the Natural 7th degree are Leading Tone instead of Sub-Tonic.
Borrowed Chords	V V Dom7	C# vi° C# vi min7♭5	D# vii° D# vii°7	D# vii min7♭5 D ♭VII Maj7

**Major Keys
Harmonic Progression
Diatonic Harmony**

Dominant Chord
Family

Sub-Dominant
Chord Family

Tonic Chord
Family

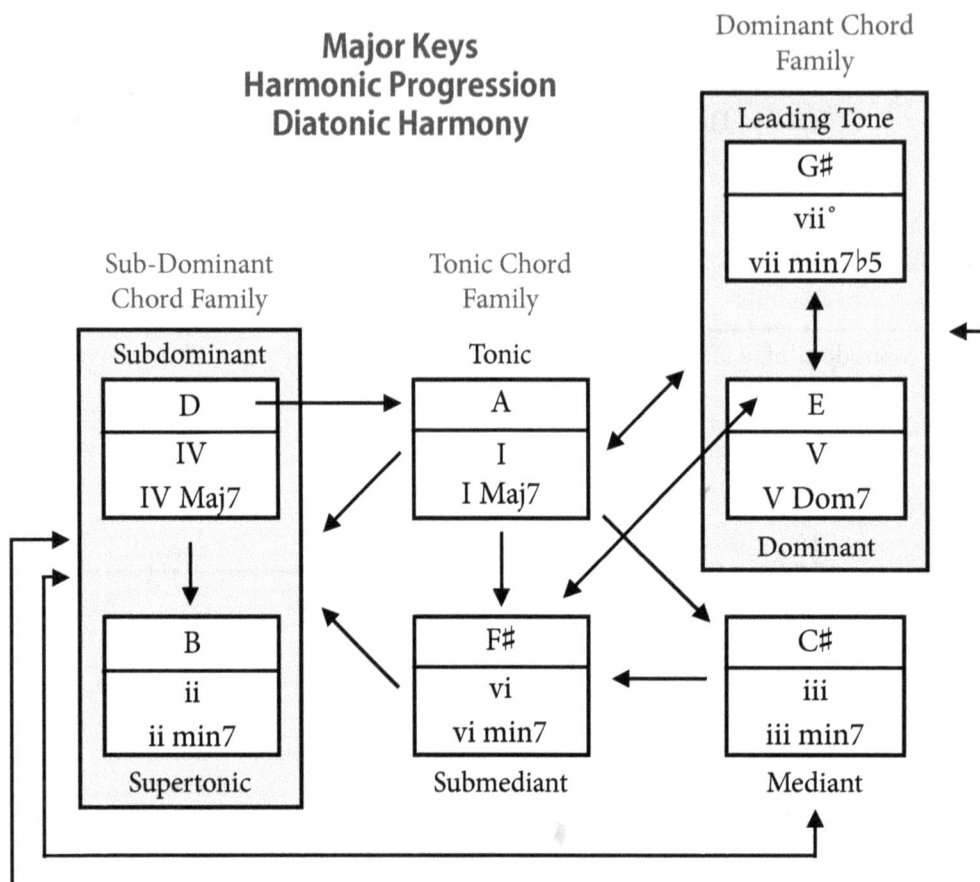

(B) ii° / ii min7♭5 can go to the (G#) vii° / vii min7♭5

(C#) iii / iii min7 can go to the (G) ♭VII / ♭VII Maj7 / ♭VII Dom7 **and vise versa**

(F#) vi / vi min7 can go to the (G) ♭VII / ♭VII Maj7 / ♭VII Dom7 **and vise versa**

Degrees	A Ionian	B Dorian	C# Phrygian	D Lydian
Harmonized Chords	M, Madd9, Madd11, M6, Sus2, Sus4, M7sus2, M7sus4, M7	m, madd9, madd11, m6, sus2, sus4, 7sus2, 7sus4, m7	m, madd11, sus4, 7sus4, m7	M, Madd9, M6, sus2, M7sus2, M7
Borrowed Chords	I Dom7	ii° ii min7♭5	iii° iii min7♭5	iv iv min/Maj7

Degrees	E Mixolydian	F# Aeolian	G# Locrian	
Harmonized Chords	M, Madd9, Madd11, M6, sus2, sus4, 7sus2, 7sus4, 7	m, madd9, madd11, sus2, sus4, 7sus2, 7sus4, m7	dim, m7♭5	Chords built off of the Flat 7th degree are Sub-Tonic instead of Leading Tone.
Borrowed Chords	v v min7	F ♭VI+ F ♭VI Maj7#5	G ♭VII G ♭VII Maj7	G ♭VII Dom7 G# vii° 7

Chord Progression Chart in Key of A Minor

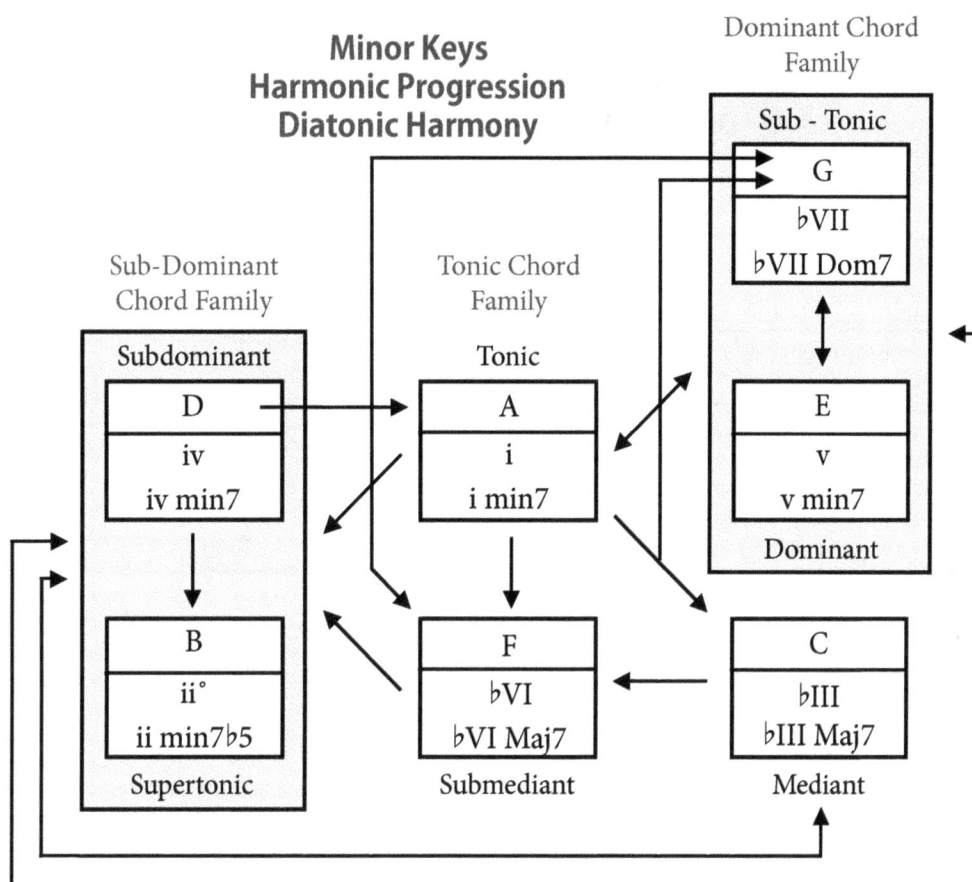

Minor Keys
Harmonic Progression
Diatonic Harmony

Dominant Chord Family

Sub-Dominant Chord Family

Tonic Chord Family

Sub - Tonic

G
♭VII
♭VII Dom7

Subdominant

D
iv
iv min7

Tonic

A
i
i min7

E
v
v min7

Dominant

B
ii°
ii min7♭5

Supertonic

F
♭VI
♭VI Maj7

Submediant

C
♭III
♭III Maj7

Mediant

(B) ii° / ii min7♭5 can go to the (G#) vii° / vii min7♭5

(F) ♭VI / ♭VI Maj7 can go to the (E) V / V Dom7 **and vise versa**

Degrees	A Aeolian	B Locrian	C Ionian	D Dorian
Harmonized Chords	m, madd9, madd11, sus2, sus4, 7sus2, 7sus4, m7	dim, m7♭5	M, Madd9, Madd11, M6, Sus2, Sus4, M7sus2, M7sus4, M7	m, madd9, madd11, m6, sus2, sus4, 7sus2, 7sus4, m7
Borrowed Chords	i min/Maj7	ii ii min7	♭III+ ♭III Maj7#5	IV IV Dom7

Degrees	E Phrygian	F Lydian	G Mixolydian	
Harmonized Chords	m, madd11, sus4, 7sus4, m7	M, Madd9, M6, sus2, M7sus2, M7	M, Madd9, Madd11, M6, sus2, sus4, 7sus2, 7sus4, 7	Chords built off of the Natural 7th degree are Leading Tone instead of Sub-Tonic.
Borrowed Chords	V V Dom7	F# vi° F# vi min7♭5	G# vii° G# vii°7	G# vii min7♭5 G ♭VII Maj7

Chord Progression Chart in Key of D Major

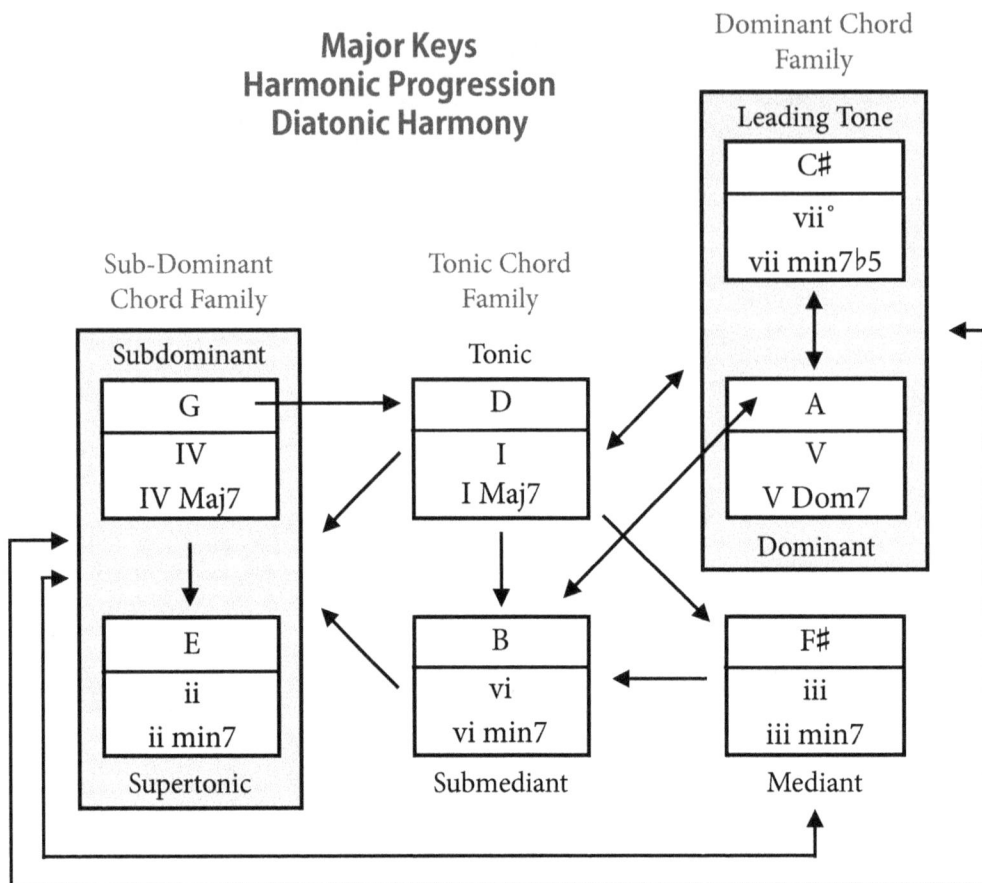

**Major Keys
Harmonic Progression
Diatonic Harmony**

Dominant Chord Family

Sub-Dominant Chord Family

Tonic Chord Family

Subdominant

G
IV
IV Maj7

Tonic

D
I
I Maj7

Leading Tone

C#
vii°
vii min7♭5

A
V
V Dom7

Dominant

E
ii
ii min7

Supertonic

B
vi
vi min7

Submediant

F#
iii
iii min7

Mediant

(E) ii° / ii min7♭5 can go to the (C#) vii° / vii min7♭5

(F#) iii / iii min7 can go to the (C) ♭VII / ♭VII Maj7 / ♭VII Dom7 **and vise versa**

(B) vi / vi min7 can go to the (C) ♭VII / ♭VII Maj7 / ♭VII Dom7 **and vise versa**

Degrees	D Ionian	E Dorian	F# Phrygian	G Lydian
Harmonized Chords	M, Madd9, Madd11, M6, Sus2, Sus4, M7sus2, M7sus4, M7	m, madd9, madd11, m6, sus2, sus4, 7sus2, 7sus4, m7	m, madd11, sus4, 7sus4, m7	M, Madd9, M6, sus2, M7sus2, M7
Borrowed Chords	I Dom7	ii° ii min7♭5	iii° iii min7♭5	iv iv min/Maj7

Degrees	A Mixolydian	B Aeolian	C# Locrian	
Harmonized Chords	M, Madd9, Madd11, M6, sus2, sus4, 7sus2, 7sus4, 7	m, madd9, madd11, sus2, sus4, 7sus2, 7sus4, m7	dim, m7♭5	Chords built off of the Flat 7th degree are Sub-Tonic instead of Leading Tone.
Borrowed Chords	v v min7	B♭ ♭VI+ B♭ ♭VI Maj7#5	C ♭VII C ♭VII Maj7	C ♭VII Dom7 C# vii° 7

Chord Progression Chart in Key of D Minor

**Minor Keys
Harmonic Progression
Diatonic Harmony**

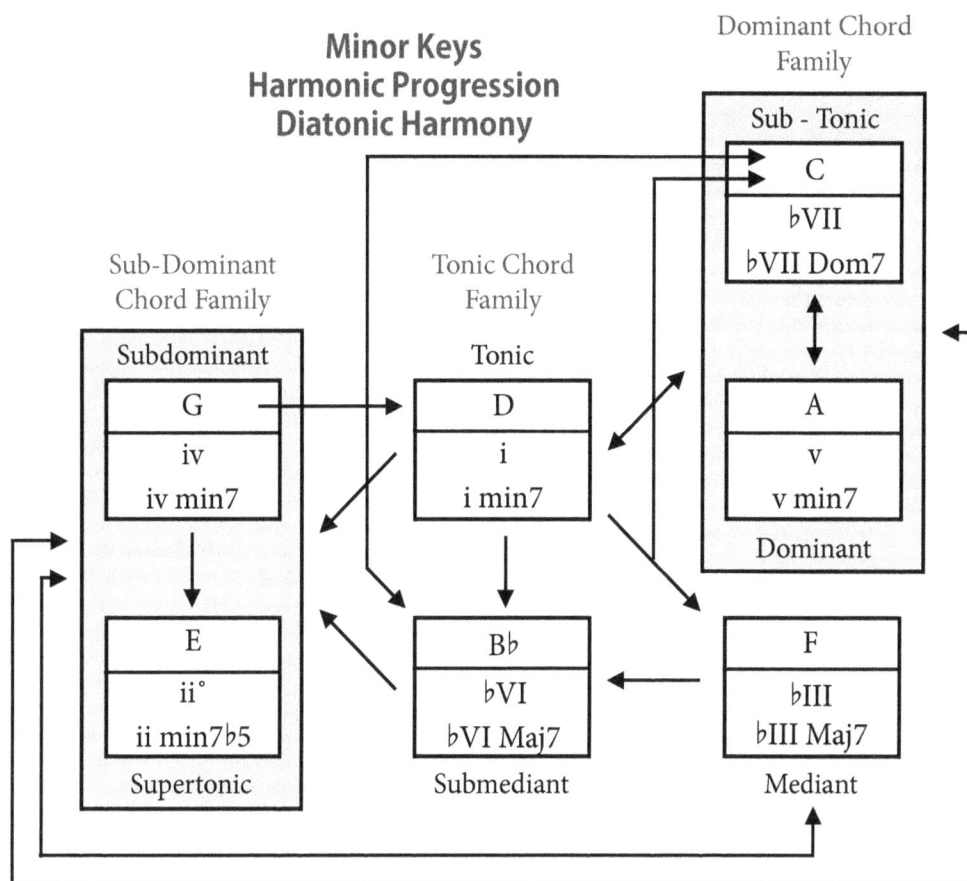

(E) ii° / ii min7♭5 can go to the (C♯) vii° / vii min7♭5

(B♭) ♭VI / ♭VI Maj7 can go to the (A) V / V Dom7 **and vise versa**

Degrees	D Aeolian	E Locrian	F Ionian	G Dorian
Harmonized Chords	m, madd9, madd11, sus2, sus4, 7sus2, 7sus4, m7	dim, m7♭5	M, Madd9, Madd11, M6, Sus2, Sus4, M7sus2, M7sus4, M7	m, madd9, madd11, m6, sus2, sus4, 7sus2, 7sus4, m7
Borrowed Chords	i min/Maj7	ii ii min7	♭III+ ♭III Maj7♯5	IV IV Dom7

Degrees	A Phrygian	B♭ Lydian	C Mixolydian	
Harmonized Chords	m, madd11, sus4, 7sus4, m7	M, Madd9, M6, sus2, M7sus2, M7	M, Madd9, Madd11, M6, sus2, sus4, 7sus2, 7sus4, 7	Chords built off of the Natural 7th degree are Leading Tone instead of Sub-Tonic.
Borrowed Chords	V V Dom7	B vi° B vi min7♭5	C♯ vii° C♯ vii°7	C♯ vii min7♭5 C ♭VII Maj7

49

Chord Progression Chart in Key of G Major

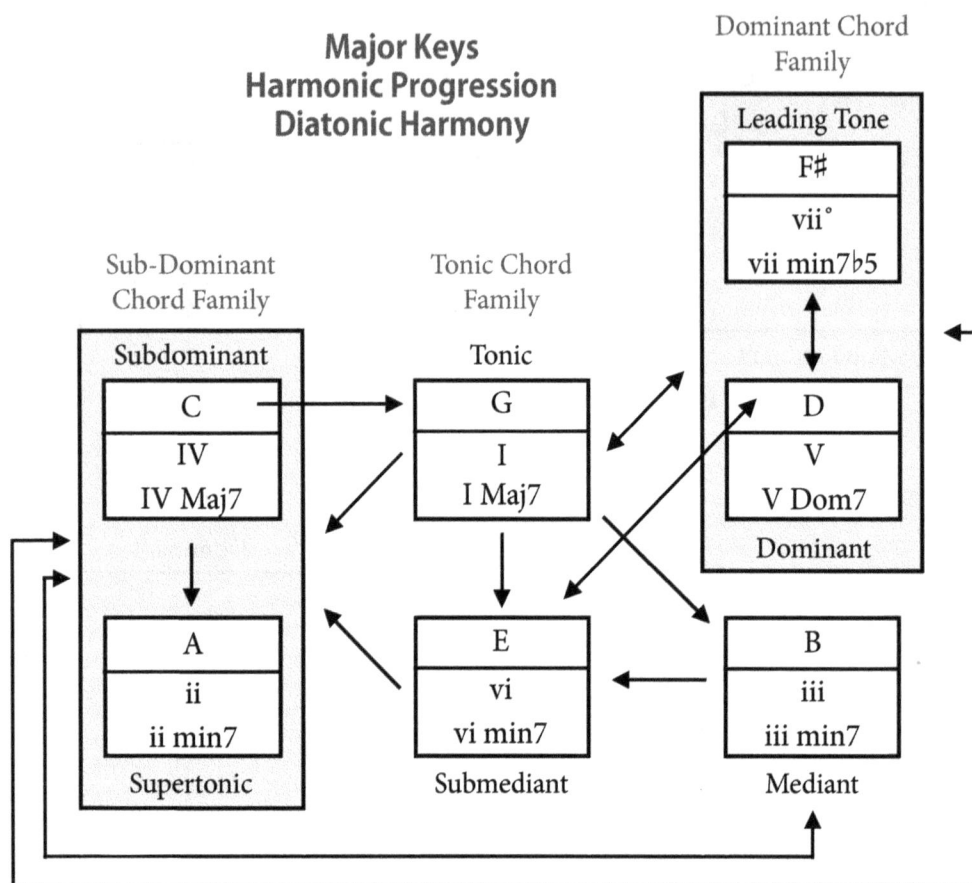

Major Keys
Harmonic Progression
Diatonic Harmony

Dominant Chord Family

Sub-Dominant Chord Family

Tonic Chord Family

Leading Tone

| F# |
| vii° |
| vii min7♭5 |

Subdominant

| C |
| IV |
| IV Maj7 |

Tonic

| G |
| I |
| I Maj7 |

| D |
| V |
| V Dom7 |

Dominant

| A |
| ii |
| ii min7 |

Supertonic

| E |
| vi |
| vi min7 |

Submediant

| B |
| iii |
| iii min7 |

Mediant

(A) ii° / ii min7♭5 can go to the (F#) vii° / vii min7♭5

(B) iii / iii min7 can go to the (F) ♭VII / ♭VII Maj7 / ♭VII Dom7 **and vise versa**

(E) vi / vi min7 can go to the (F) ♭VII / ♭VII Maj7 / ♭VII Dom7 **and vise versa**

Degrees	G Ionian	A Dorian	B Phrygian	C Lydian
Harmonized Chords	M, Madd9, Madd11, M6, Sus2, Sus4, M7sus2, M7sus4, M7	m, madd9, madd11, m6, sus2, sus4, 7sus2, 7sus4, m7	m, madd11, sus4, 7sus4, m7	M, Madd9, M6, sus2, M7sus2, M7
Borrowed Chords	I Dom7	ii° ii min7♭5	iii° iii min7♭5	iv iv min/Maj7

Degrees	D Mixolydian	E Aeolian	F# Locrian	
Harmonized Chords	M, Madd9, Madd11, M6, sus2, sus4, 7sus2, 7sus4, 7	m, madd9, madd11, sus2, sus4, 7sus2, 7sus4, m7	dim, m7♭5	Chords built off of the Flat 7th degree are Sub-Tonic instead of Leading Tone.
Borrowed Chords	v v min7	E♭ ♭VI+ E♭ ♭VI Maj7#5	F ♭VII F ♭VII Maj7	F ♭VII Dom7 F# vii° 7

Chord Progression Chart in Key of G Minor

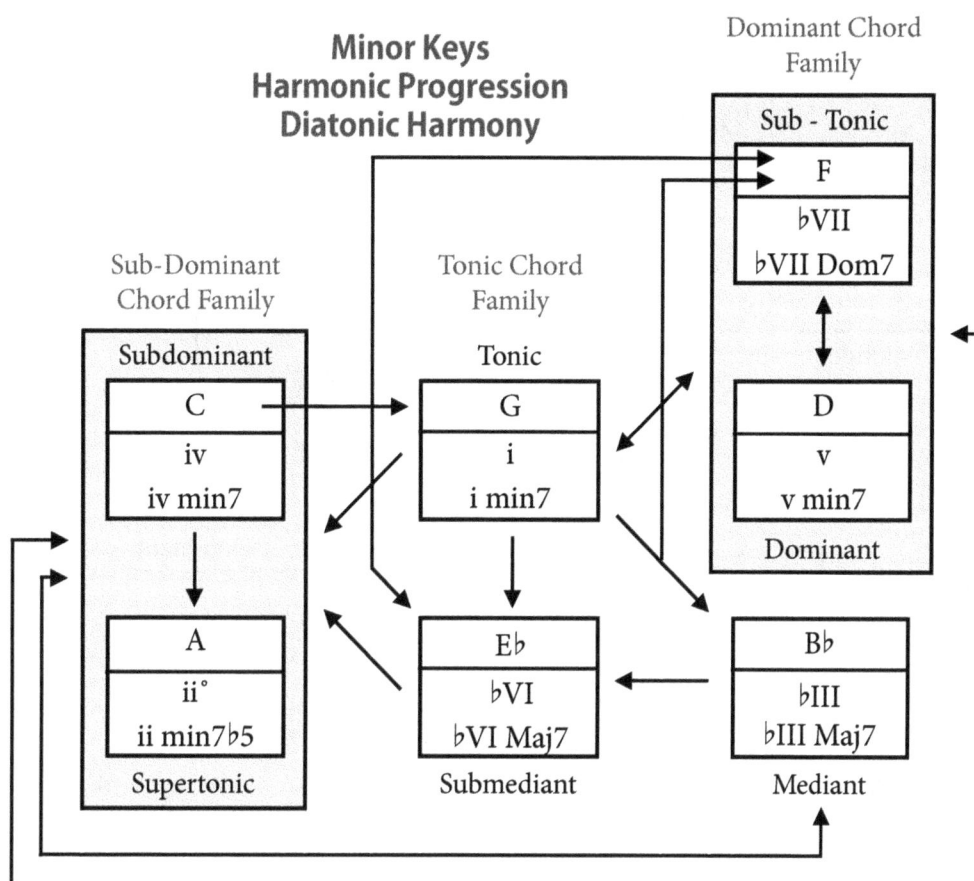

**Minor Keys
Harmonic Progression
Diatonic Harmony**

(A) ii° / ii min7♭5 can go to the (F♯) vii° / vii min7♭5

(E♭) ♭VI / ♭VI Maj7 can go to the (D) V / V Dom7 **and vise versa**

Degrees	G Aeolian	A Locrian	B♭ Ionian	C Dorian
Harmonized Chords	m, madd9, madd11, sus2, sus4, 7sus2, 7sus4, m7	dim, m7♭5	M, Madd9, Madd11, M6, Sus2, Sus4, M7sus2, M7sus4, M7	m, madd9, madd11, m6, sus2, sus4, 7sus2, 7sus4, m7
Borrowed Chords	i min/Maj7	ii ii min7	♭III+ ♭III Maj7♯5	IV IV Dom7

Degrees	D Phrygian	E♭ Lydian	F Mixolydian	
Harmonized Chords	m, madd11, sus4, 7sus4, m7	M, Madd9, M6, sus2, M7sus2, M7	M, Madd9, Madd11, M6, sus2, sus4, 7sus2, 7sus4, 7	Chords built off of the Natural 7th degree are Leading Tone instead of Sub-Tonic.
Borrowed Chords	V V Dom7	E vi° E vi min7♭5	F♯ vii° F♯ vii°7	F♯ vii min7♭5 F ♭VII Maj7

51

Chord Progression Chart in Key of C Major

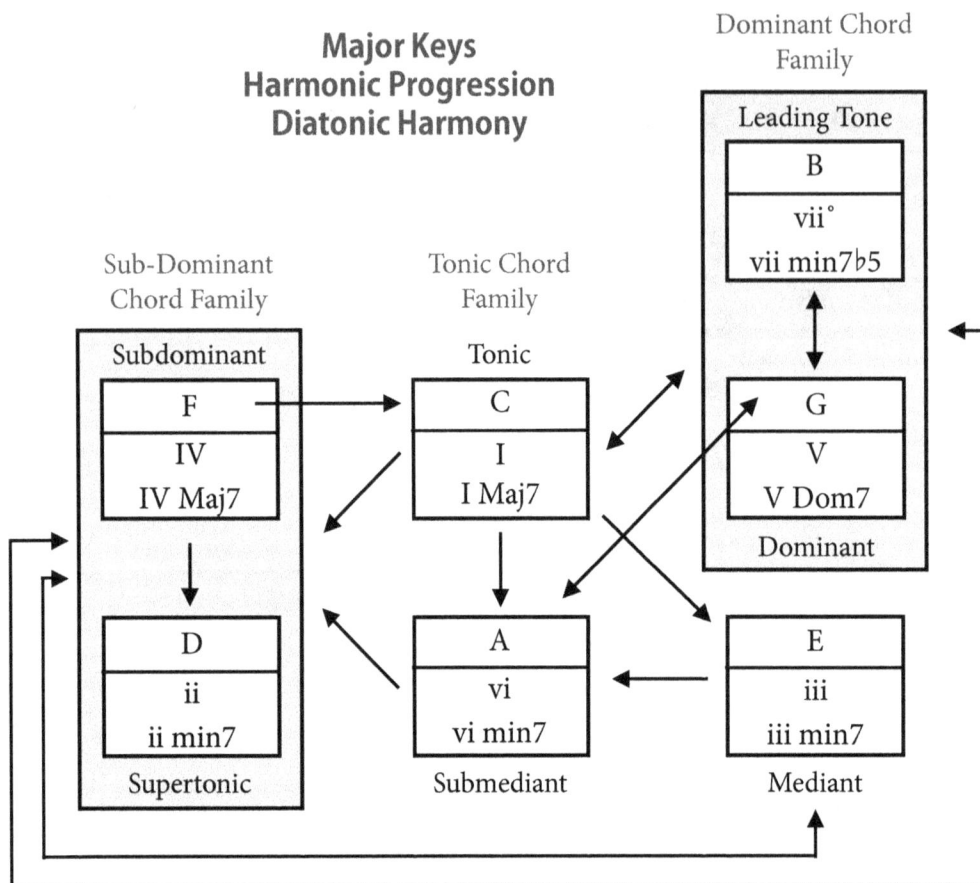

Major Keys
Harmonic Progression
Diatonic Harmony

Dominant Chord Family

Sub-Dominant Chord Family

Tonic Chord Family

Leading Tone

B
vii°
vii min7♭5

Subdominant

F
IV
IV Maj7

Tonic

C
I
I Maj7

G
V
V Dom7

Dominant

D
ii
ii min7

Supertonic

A
vi
vi min7

Submediant

E
iii
iii min7

Mediant

(D) ii° / ii min7♭5 can go to the (B) vii° / vii min7♭5

(E) iii / iii min7 can go to the (B♭) ♭VII / ♭VII Maj7 / ♭VII Dom7 **and vise versa**

(A) vi / vi min7 can go to the (B♭) ♭VII / ♭VII Maj7 / ♭VII Dom7 **and vise versa**

Degrees	C Ionian	D Dorian	E Phrygian	F Lydian
Harmonized Chords	M, Madd9, Madd11, M6, Sus2, Sus4, M7sus2, M7sus4, M7	m, madd9, madd11, m6, sus2, sus4, 7sus2, 7sus4, m7	m, madd11, sus4, 7sus4, m7	M, Madd9, M6, sus2, M7sus2, M7
Borrowed Chords	I Dom7	ii° ii min7♭5	iii° iii min7♭5	iv iv min/Maj7

Degrees	G Mixolydian	A Aeolian	B Locrian	
Harmonized Chords	M, Madd9, Madd11, M6, sus2, sus4, 7sus2, 7sus4, 7	m, madd9, madd11, sus2, sus4, 7sus2, 7sus4, m7	dim, m7♭5	Chords built off of the Flat 7th degree are Sub-Tonic instead of Leading Tone.
Borrowed Chords	v v min7	A♭ ♭VI+ A♭ ♭VI Maj7♯5	B♭ ♭VII B♭ ♭VII Maj7	B♭ ♭VII Dom7 B vii° 7

**Minor Keys
Harmonic Progression
Diatonic Harmony**

Dominant Chord
Family

Sub-Dominant
Chord Family

Tonic Chord
Family

Sub - Tonic

| Bb |
| $\flat$VII |
| $\flat$VII Dom7 |

Subdominant

| F |
| iv |
| iv min7 |

Tonic

| C |
| i |
| i min7 |

| G |
| v |
| v min7 |

Dominant

| D |
| ii° |
| ii min7$\flat$5 |

Supertonic

| A$\flat$ |
| $\flat$VI |
| $\flat$VI Maj7 |

Submediant

| E$\flat$ |
| $\flat$III |
| $\flat$III Maj7 |

Mediant

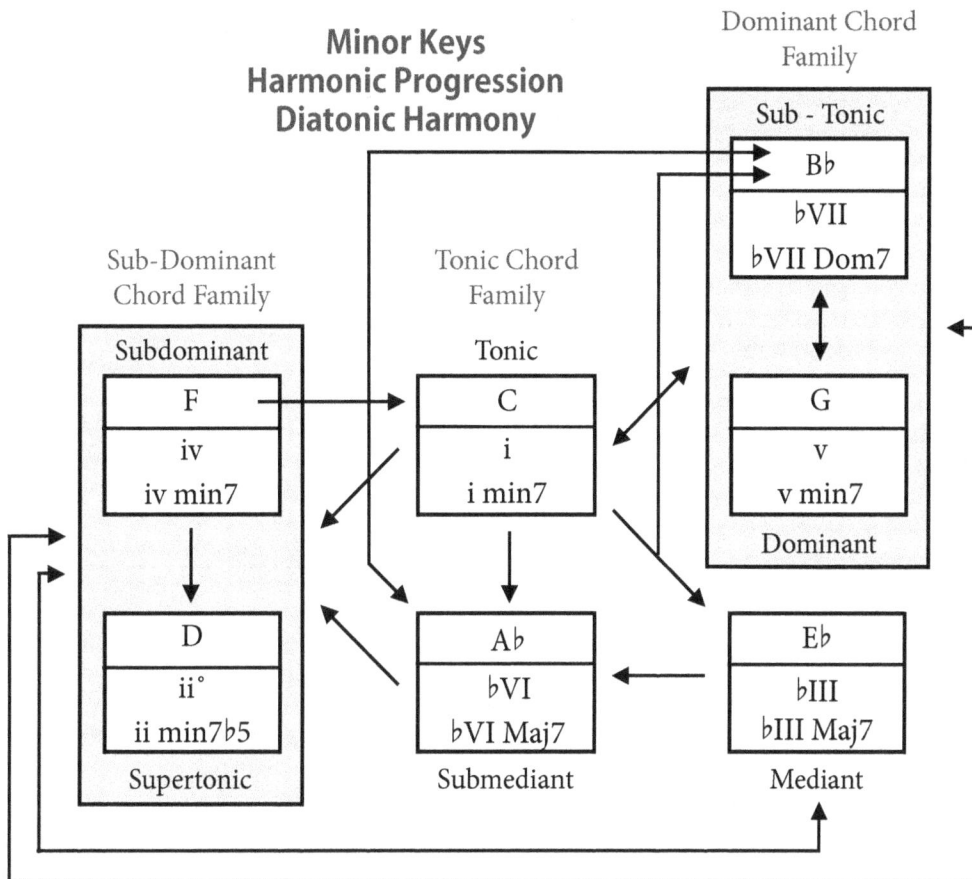

(D) ii° / ii min7$\flat$5 can go to the (B) vii° / vii min7$\flat$5

(A$\flat$) $\flat$VI / $\flat$VI Maj7 can go to the (G) V / V Dom7 **and vise versa**

Degrees	C Aeolian	D Locrian	E$\flat$ Ionian	F Dorian
Harmonized Chords	m, madd9, madd11, sus2, sus4, 7sus2, 7sus4, m7	dim, m7$\flat$5	M, Madd9, Madd11, M6, Sus2, Sus4, M7sus2, M7sus4, M7	m, madd9, madd11, m6, sus2, sus4, 7sus2, 7sus4, m7
Borrowed Chords	i min/Maj7	ii ii min7	$\flat$III+ $\flat$III Maj7#5	IV IV Dom7
Degrees	G Phrygian	A$\flat$ Lydian	B$\flat$ Mixolydian	
Harmonized Chords	m, madd11, sus4, 7sus4, m7	M, Madd9, M6, sus2, M7sus2, M7	M, Madd9, Madd11, M6, sus2, sus4, 7sus2, 7sus4, 7	Chords built off of the Natural 7th degree are Leading Tone instead of Sub-Tonic.
Borrowed Chords	V V Dom7	A vi° A vi min7$\flat$5	B vii° B vii°7	B vii min7$\flat$5 B$\flat$ $\flat$VII Maj7

Chord Progression Chart in Key of F Major

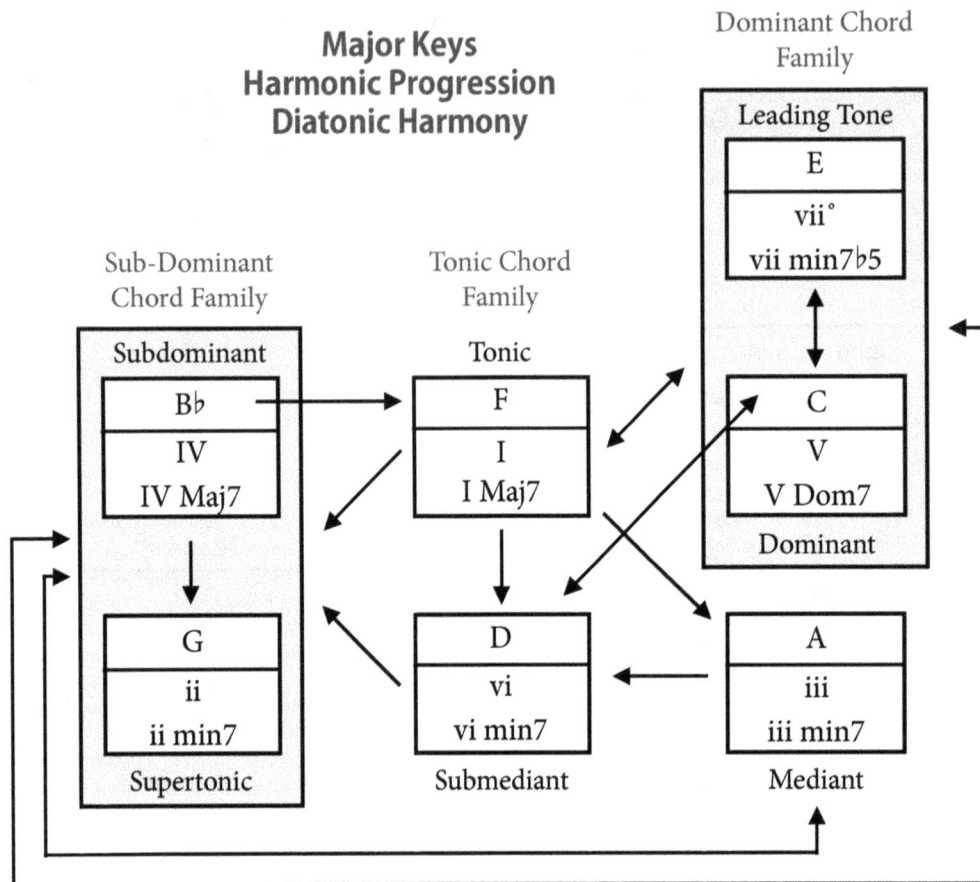

Major Keys
Harmonic Progression
Diatonic Harmony

Dominant Chord
Family

Sub-Dominant
Chord Family

Tonic Chord
Family

Leading Tone

E
vii°
vii min7♭5

Subdominant

B♭
IV
IV Maj7

Tonic

F
I
I Maj7

C
V
V Dom7

Dominant

G
ii
ii min7

Supertonic

D
vi
vi min7

Submediant

A
iii
iii min7

Mediant

(G) ii° / ii min7♭5 can go to the (E) vii° / vii min7♭5

(A) iii / iii min7 can go to the (E♭) ♭VII / ♭VII Maj7 / ♭VII Dom7 **and vise versa**

(D) vi / vi min7 can go to the (E♭) ♭VII / ♭VII Maj7 / ♭VII Dom7 **and vise versa**

Degrees	F Ionian	G Dorian	A Phrygian	B♭ Lydian
Harmonized Chords	M, Madd9, Madd11, M6, Sus2, Sus4, M7sus2, M7sus4, M7	m, madd9, madd11, m6, sus2, sus4, 7sus2, 7sus4, m7	m, madd11, sus4, 7sus4, m7	M, Madd9, M6, sus2, M7sus2, M7
Borrowed Chords	I Dom7	ii° ii min7♭5	iii° iii min7♭5	iv iv min/Maj7
Degrees	C Mixolydian	D Aeolian	E Locrian	
Harmonized Chords	M, Madd9, Madd11, M6, sus2, sus4, 7sus2, 7sus4, 7	m, madd9, madd11, sus2, sus4, 7sus2, 7sus4, m7	dim, m7♭5	Chords built off of the Flat 7th degree are Sub-Tonic instead of Leading Tone.
Borrowed Chords	v v min7	D♭　♭VI+ D♭　♭VI Maj7♯5	E♭　♭VII E♭　♭VII Maj7	E♭　♭VII Dom7 E　vii° 7

Chord Progression Chart in Key of F Minor

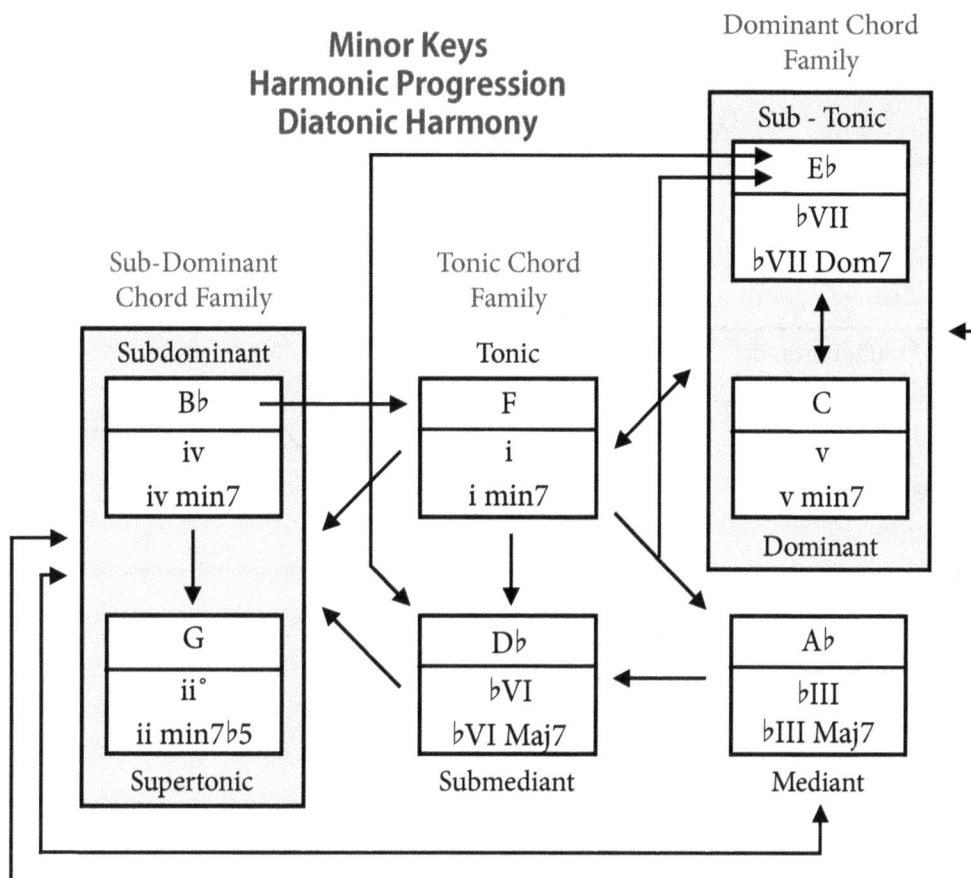

Minor Keys
Harmonic Progression
Diatonic Harmony

Dominant Chord
Family

Sub-Dominant
Chord Family

Tonic Chord
Family

Sub - Tonic

Eb
bVII
bVII Dom7

Subdominant

Bb
iv
iv min7

Tonic

F
i
i min7

C
v
v min7

Dominant

G
ii°
ii min7b5

Supertonic

Db
bVI
bVI Maj7

Submediant

Ab
bIII
bIII Maj7

Mediant

(G) ii° / ii min7b5 can go to the (E) vii° / vii min7b5

(Db) bVI / bVI Maj7 can go to the (C) V / V Dom7 **and vise versa**

Degrees	F Aeolian	G Locrian	Ab Ionian	Bb Dorian
Harmonized Chords	m, madd9, madd11, sus2, sus4, 7sus2, 7sus4, m7	dim, m7b5	M, Madd9, Madd11, M6, Sus2, Sus4, M7sus2, M7sus4, M7	m, madd9, madd11, m6, sus2, sus4, 7sus2, 7sus4, m7
Borrowed Chords	i min/Maj7	ii ii min7	bIII+ bIII Maj7#5	IV IV Dom7
Degrees	C Phrygian	Db Lydian	Eb Mixolydian	
Harmonized Chords	m, madd11, sus4, 7sus4, m7	M, Madd9, M6, sus2, M7sus2, M7	M, Madd9, Madd11, M6, sus2, sus4, 7sus2, 7sus4, 7	Chords built off of the Natural 7th degree are Leading Tone instead of Sub-Tonic.
Borrowed Chords	V V Dom7	D vi° D vi min7b5	E vii° E vii°7	E vii min7b5 Eb bVII Maj7

**Major Keys
Harmonic Progression
Diatonic Harmony**

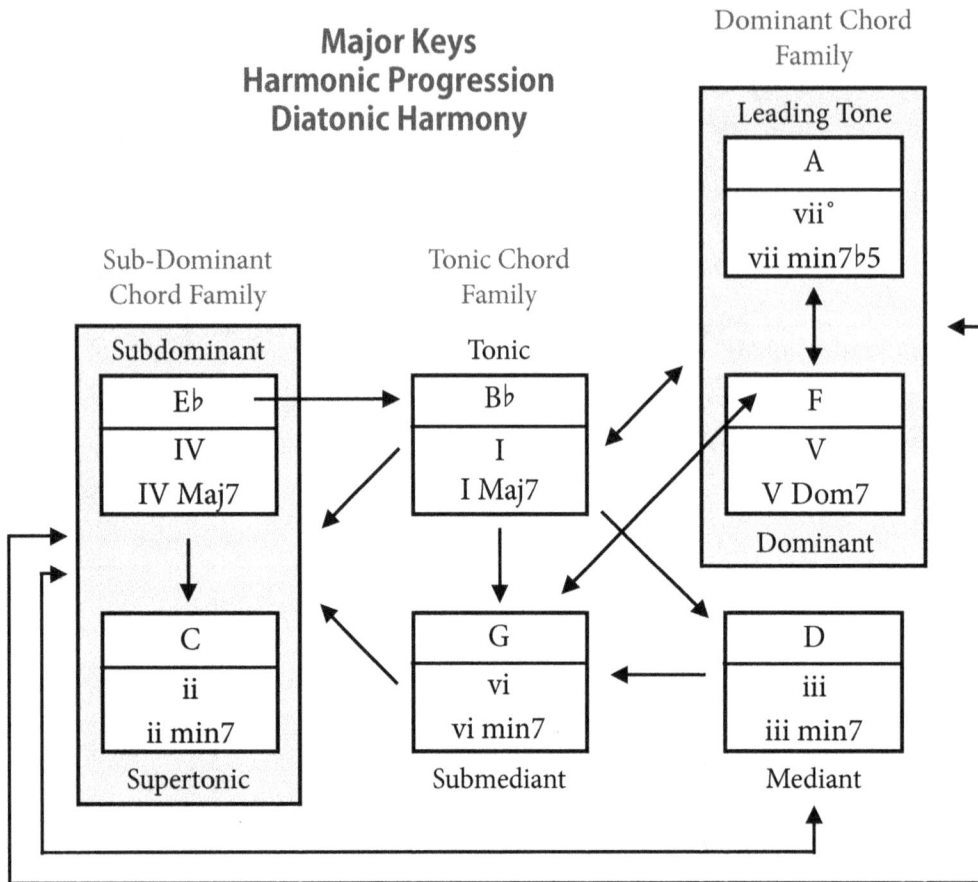

(C) ii° / ii min7♭5 can go to the (A) vii° / vii min7♭5

(D) iii / iii min7 can go to the (A♭) ♭VII / ♭VII Maj7 / ♭VII Dom7 **and vise versa**

(G) vi / vi min7 can go to the (A♭) ♭VII / ♭VII Maj7 / ♭VII Dom7 **and vise versa**

Degrees	B♭ Ionian	C Dorian	D Phrygian	E♭ Lydian
Harmonized Chords	M, Madd9, Madd11, M6, Sus2, Sus4, M7sus2, M7sus4, M7	m, madd9, madd11, m6, sus2, sus4, 7sus2, 7sus4, m7	m, madd11, sus4, 7sus4, m7	M, Madd9, M6, sus2, M7sus2, M7
Borrowed Chords	I Dom7	ii° ii min7♭5	iii° iii min7♭5	iv iv min/Maj7
Degrees	F Mixolydian	G Aeolian	A Locrian	
Harmonized Chords	M, Madd9, Madd11, M6, sus2, sus4, 7sus2, 7sus4, 7	m, madd9, madd11, sus2, sus4, 7sus2, 7sus4, m7	dim, m7♭5	Chords built off of the Flat 7th degree are Sub-Tonic instead of Leading Tone.
Borrowed Chords	v v min7	G♭ ♭VI+ G♭ ♭VI Maj7#5	A♭ ♭VII A♭ ♭VII Maj7	A♭ ♭VII Dom7 A vii° 7

Chord Progression Chart in Key of B♭ Minor

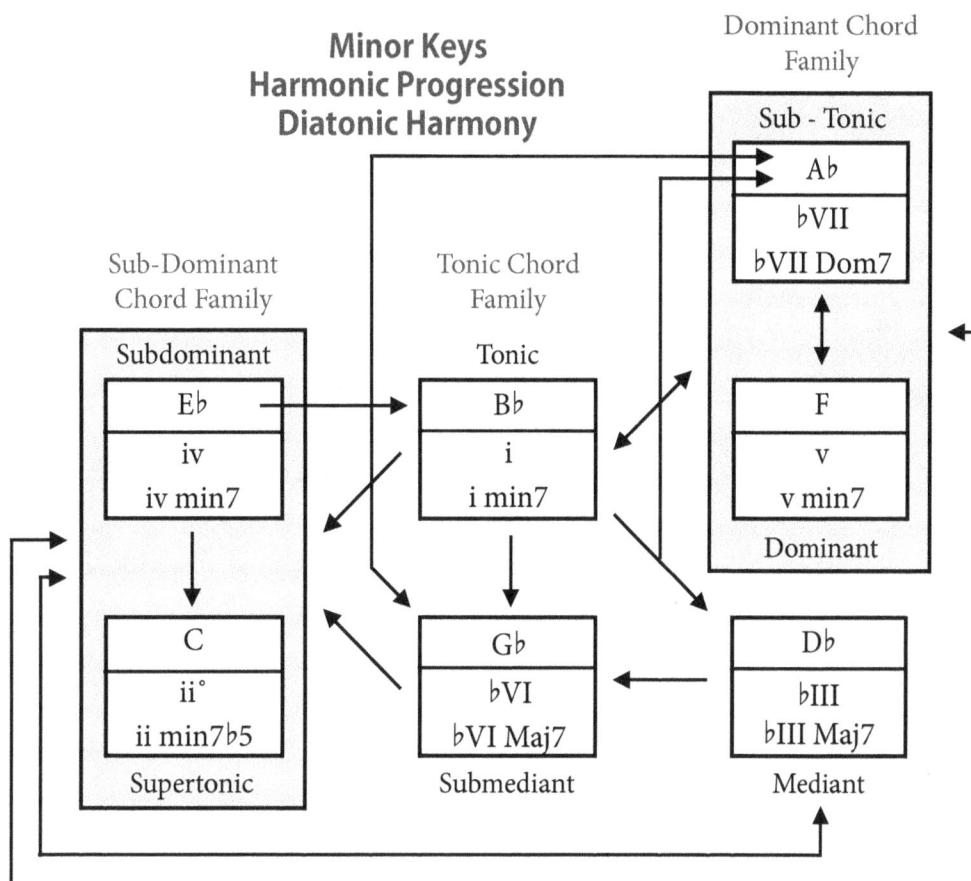

**Minor Keys
Harmonic Progression
Diatonic Harmony**

Dominant Chord Family

Sub-Dominant Chord Family

Tonic Chord Family

Sub - Tonic

A♭
♭VII
♭VII Dom7

Subdominant

E♭
iv
iv min7

Tonic

B♭
i
i min7

F
v
v min7

Dominant

C
ii°
ii min7♭5

Supertonic

G♭
♭VI
♭VI Maj7

Submediant

D♭
♭III
♭III Maj7

Mediant

(C) ii° / ii min7♭5 can go to the (A) vii° / vii min7♭5

(G♭) ♭VI / ♭VI Maj7 can go to the (F) V / V Dom7 **and vise versa**

Degrees	B♭ Aeolian	C Locrian	D♭ Ionian	E♭ Dorian
Harmonized Chords	m, madd9, madd11, sus2, sus4, 7sus2, 7sus4, m7	dim, m7♭5	M, Madd9, Madd11, M6, Sus2, Sus4, M7sus2, M7sus4, M7	m, madd9, madd11, m6, sus2, sus4, 7sus2, 7sus4, m7
Borrowed Chords	i min/Maj7	ii ii min7	♭III+ ♭III Maj7#5	IV IV Dom7

Degrees	F Phrygian	G♭ Lydian	A♭ Mixolydian	
Harmonized Chords	m, madd11, sus4, 7sus4, m7	M, Madd9, M6, sus2, M7sus2, M7	M, Madd9, Madd11, M6, sus2, sus4, 7sus2, 7sus4, 7	Chords built off of the Natural 7th degree are Leading Tone instead of Sub-Tonic.
Borrowed Chords	V V Dom7	G vi° G vi min7♭5	A vii° A vii°7	A vii min7♭5 A♭ ♭VII Maj7

Chord Progression Chart in Key of E♭ Major

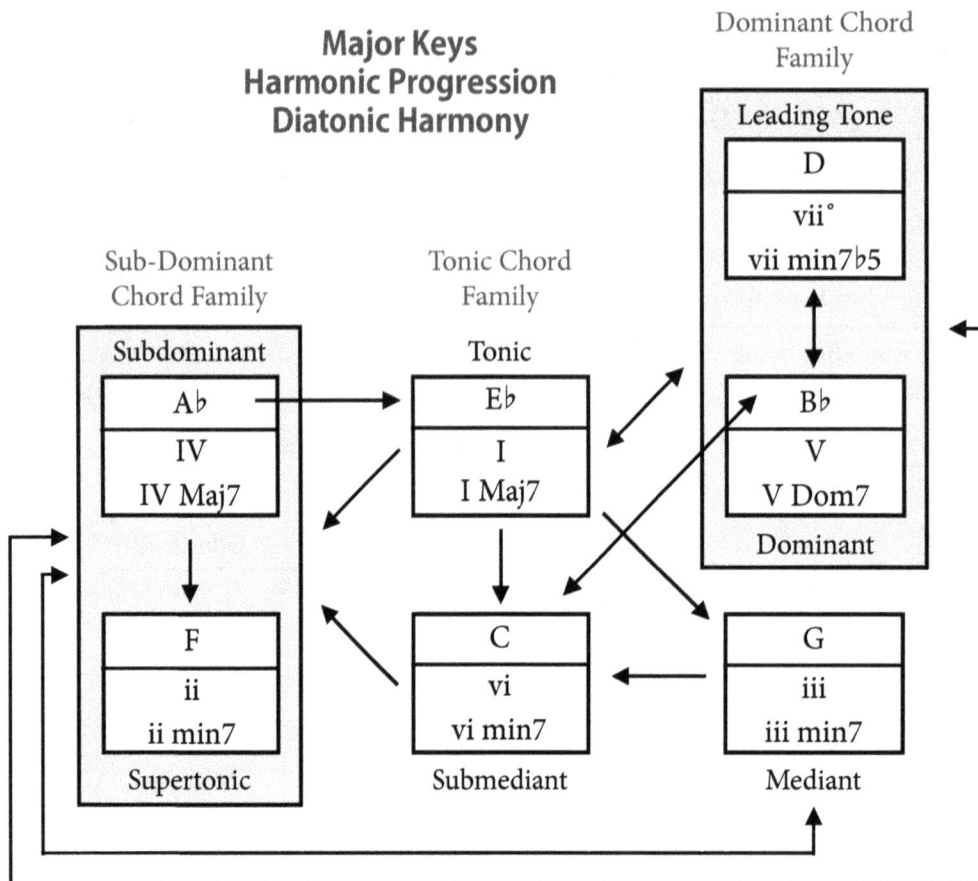

Major Keys
Harmonic Progression
Diatonic Harmony

Sub-Dominant
Chord Family

Tonic Chord
Family

Dominant Chord
Family

Leading Tone

D
vii°
vii min7♭5

Subdominant

A♭
IV
IV Maj7

Tonic

E♭
I
I Maj7

B♭
V
V Dom7

Dominant

F
ii
ii min7

Supertonic

C
vi
vi min7

Submediant

G
iii
iii min7

Mediant

(F) ii° / ii min7♭5 can go to the (D) vii° / vii min7♭5

(G) iii / iii min7 can go to the (D♭) ♭VII / ♭VII Maj7 / ♭VII Dom7 **and vise versa**

(C) vi / vi min7 can go to the (D♭) ♭VII / ♭VII Maj7 / ♭VII Dom7 **and vise versa**

Degrees	E♭ Ionian	F Dorian	G Phrygian	A♭ Lydian
Harmonized Chords	M, Madd9, Madd11, M6, Sus2, Sus4, M7sus2, M7sus4, M7	m, madd9, madd11, m6, sus2, sus4, 7sus2, 7sus4, m7	m, madd11, sus4, 7sus4, m7	M, Madd9, M6, sus2, M7sus2, M7
Borrowed Chords	I Dom7	ii° ii min7♭5	iii° iii min7♭5	iv iv min/Maj7

Degrees	B♭ Mixolydian	C Aeolian	D Locrian	
Harmonized Chords	M, Madd9, Madd11, M6, sus2, sus4, 7sus2, 7sus4, 7	m, madd9, madd11, sus2, sus4, 7sus2, 7sus4, m7	dim, m7♭5	Chords built off of the Flat 7th degree are Sub-Tonic instead of Leading Tone.
Borrowed Chords	v v min7	C♭ ♭VI+ C♭ ♭VI Maj7#5	D♭ ♭VII D♭ ♭VII Maj7	D♭ ♭VII Dom7 D vii° 7

**Minor Keys
Harmonic Progression
Diatonic Harmony**

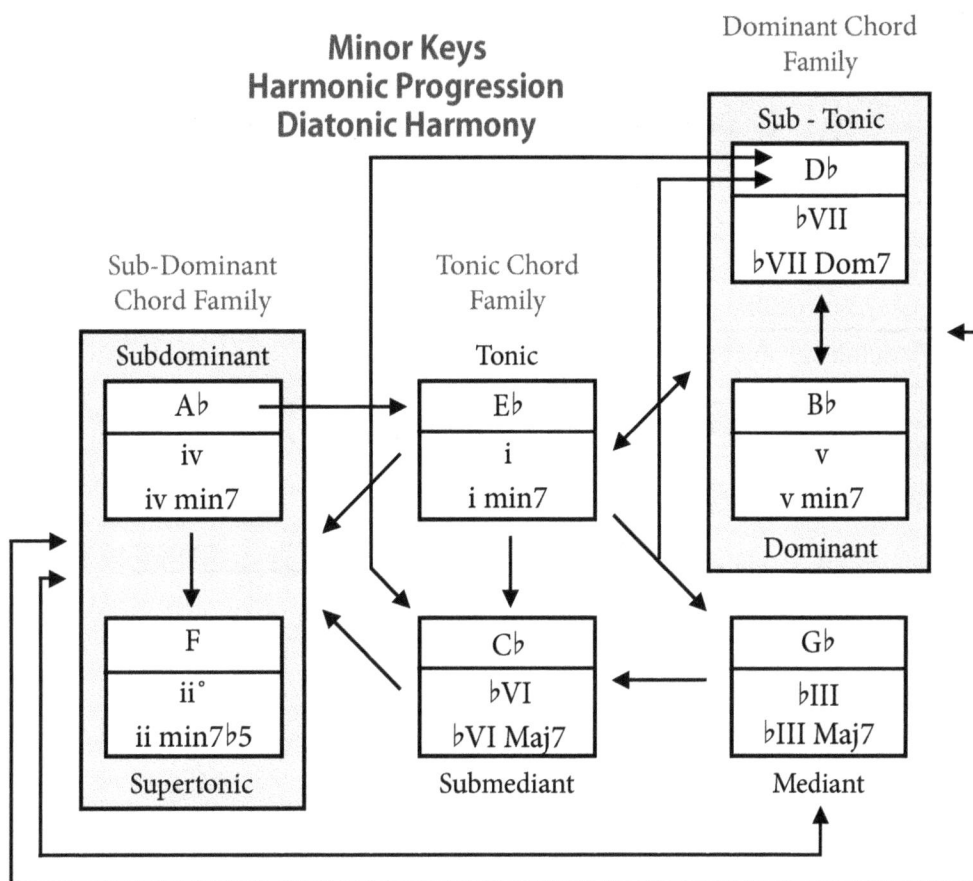

(F) ii° / ii min7♭5 can go to the (D) vii° / vii min7♭5

(C♭) ♭VI / ♭VI Maj7 can go to the (B♭) V / V Dom7 **and vise versa**

Degrees	E♭ Aeolian	F Locrian	G♭ Ionian	A♭ Dorian
Harmonized Chords	m, madd9, madd11, sus2, sus4, 7sus2, 7sus4, m7	dim, m7♭5	M, Madd9, Madd11, M6, Sus2, Sus4, M7sus2, M7sus4, M7	m, madd9, madd11, m6, sus2, sus4, 7sus2, 7sus4, m7
Borrowed Chords	i min/Maj7	ii ii min7	♭III+ ♭III Maj7#5	IV IV Dom7

Degrees	B♭ Phrygian	C♭ Lydian	D♭ Mixolydian	
Harmonized Chords	m, madd11, sus4, 7sus4, m7	M, Madd9, M6, sus2, M7sus2, M7	M, Madd9, Madd11, M6, sus2, sus4, 7sus2, 7sus4, 7	Chords built off of the Natural 7th degree are Leading Tone instead of Sub-Tonic.
Borrowed Chords	V V Dom7	C vi° C vi min7♭5	D vii° D vii°7	D vii min7♭5 D♭ ♭VII Maj7

Chord Progression Chart in Key of A♭ Major

Major Keys
Harmonic Progression
Diatonic Harmony

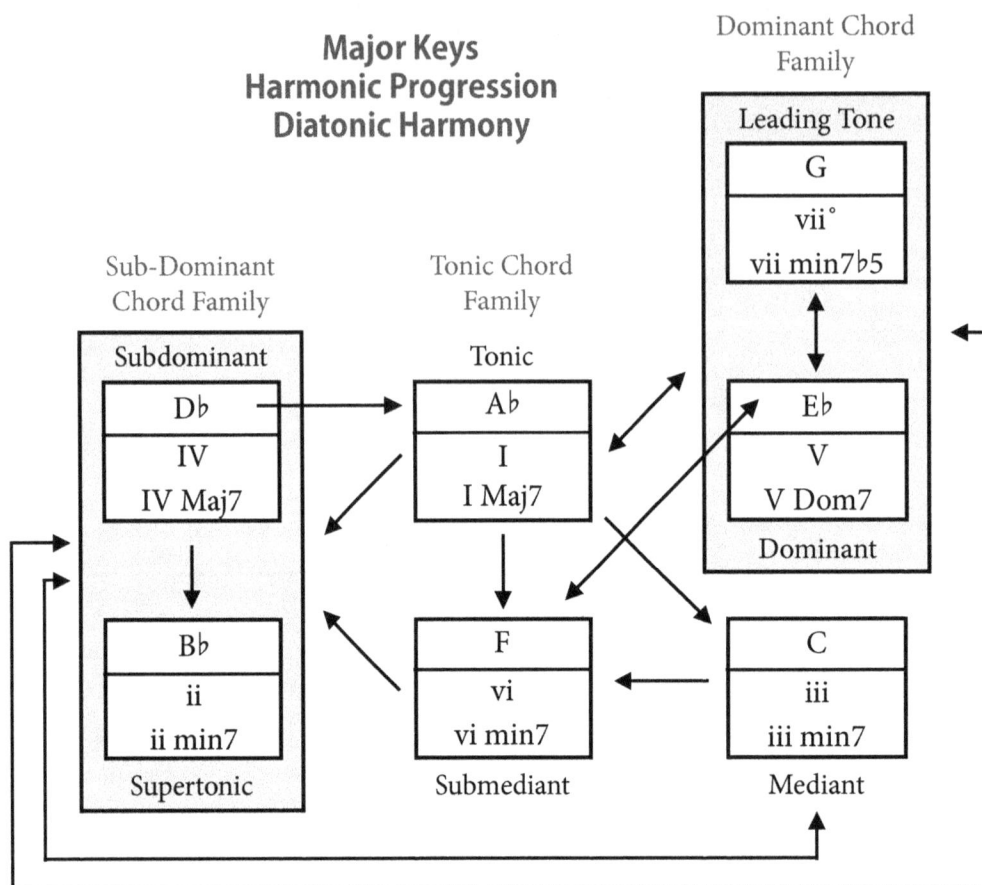

(B♭) ii° / ii min7♭5 can go to the (G) vii° / vii min7♭5

(C) iii / iii min7 can go to the (G♭) ♭VII / ♭VII Maj7 / ♭VII Dom7 **and vise versa**

(F) vi / vi min7 can go to the (G♭) ♭VII / ♭VII Maj7 / ♭VII Dom7 **and vise versa**

Degrees	A♭ Ionian	B♭ Dorian	C Phrygian	D♭ Lydian
Harmonized Chords	M, Madd9, Madd11, M6, Sus2, Sus4, M7sus2, M7sus4, M7	m, madd9, madd11, m6, sus2, sus4, 7sus2, 7sus4, m7	m, madd11, sus4, 7sus4, m7	M, Madd9, M6, sus2, M7sus2, M7
Borrowed Chords	I Dom7	ii° ii min7♭5	iii° iii min7♭5	iv iv min/Maj7

Degrees	E♭ Mixolydian	F Aeolian	G Locrian	
Harmonized Chords	M, Madd9, Madd11, M6, sus2, sus4, 7sus2, 7sus4, 7	m, madd9, madd11, sus2, sus4, 7sus2, 7sus4, m7	dim, m7♭5	Chords built off of the Flat 7th degree are Sub-Tonic instead of Leading Tone.
Borrowed Chords	v v min7	F♭ ♭VI+ F♭ ♭VI Maj7♯5	G♭ ♭VII G♭ ♭VII Maj7	G♭ ♭VII Dom7 G vii° 7

Chord Progression Chart in Key of A♭ Minor

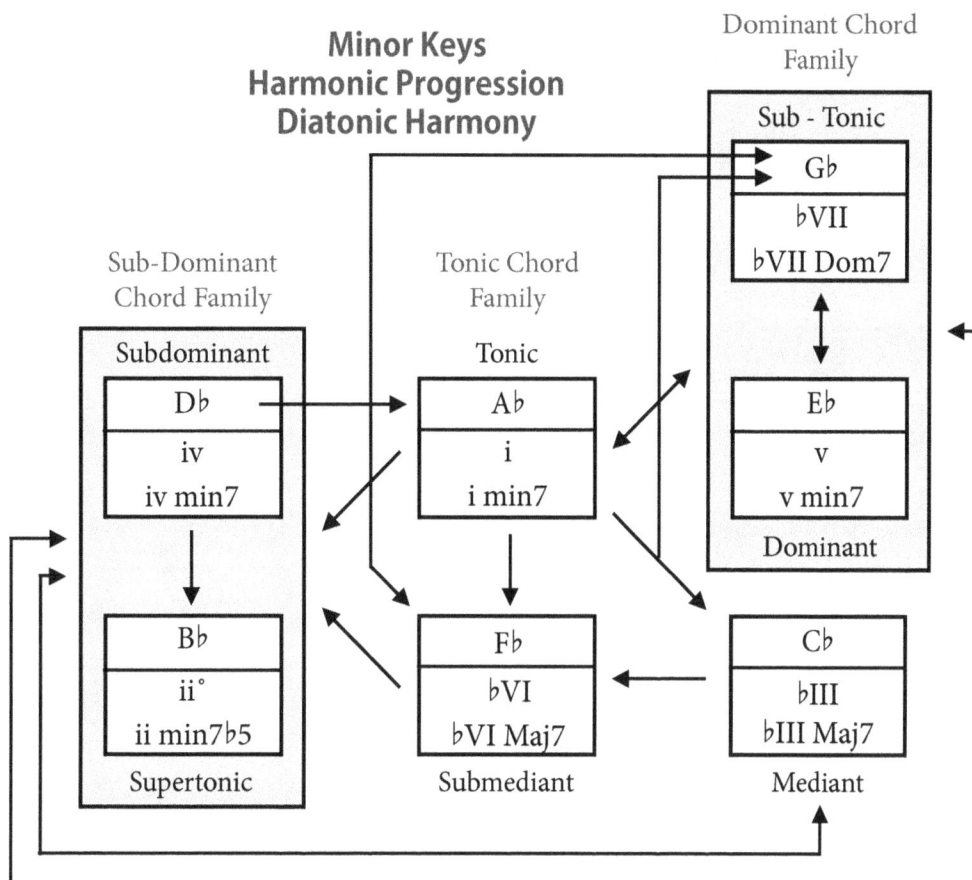

Minor Keys
Harmonic Progression
Diatonic Harmony

Dominant Chord Family

Sub-Tonic

G♭
♭VII
♭VII Dom7

Sub-Dominant Chord Family

Tonic Chord Family

Subdominant

D♭
iv
iv min7

Tonic

A♭
i
i min7

E♭
v
v min7

Dominant

B♭
ii°
ii min7♭5

Supertonic

F♭
♭VI
♭VI Maj7

Submediant

C♭
♭III
♭III Maj7

Mediant

(B♭) ii° / ii min7♭5 can go to the (G) vii° / vii min7♭5

(F♭) ♭VI / ♭VI Maj7 can go to the (E♭) V / V Dom7 and vise versa

Degrees	A♭ Aeolian	B♭ Locrian	C♭ Ionian	D♭ Dorian
Harmonized Chords	m, madd9, madd11, sus2, sus4, 7sus2, 7sus4, m7	dim, m7♭5	M, Madd9, Madd11, M6, Sus2, Sus4, M7sus2, M7sus4, M7	m, madd9, madd11, m6, sus2, sus4, 7sus2, 7sus4, m7
Borrowed Chords	i min/Maj7	ii ii min7	♭III+ ♭III Maj7#5	IV IV Dom7

Degrees	E♭ Phrygian	F♭ Lydian	G♭ Mixolydian	
Harmonized Chords	m, madd11, sus4, 7sus4, m7	M, Madd9, M6, sus2, M7sus2, M7	M, Madd9, Madd11, M6, sus2, sus4, 7sus2, 7sus4, 7	Chords built off of the Natural 7th degree are Leading Tone instead of Sub-Tonic.
Borrowed Chords	V V Dom7	F vi° F vi min7♭5	G vii° G vii°7	G vii min7♭5 G♭ ♭VII Maj7

Chord Progression Chart in Key of D♭ Major

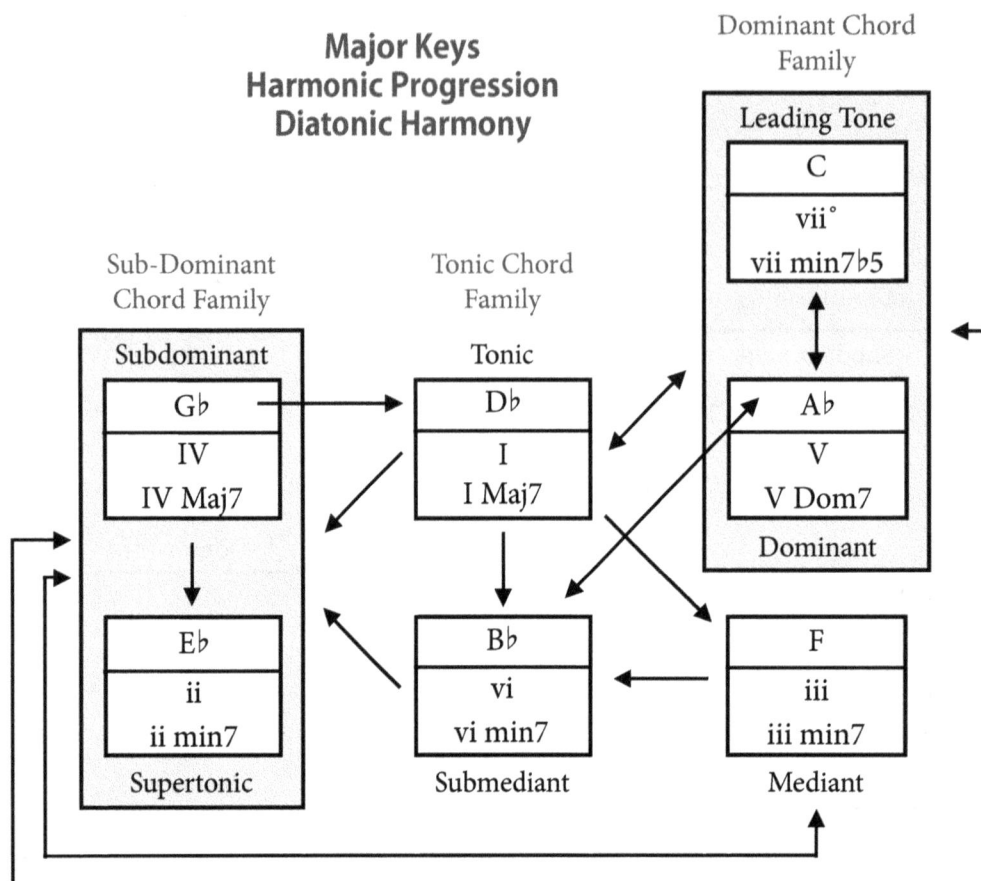

Major Keys
Harmonic Progression
Diatonic Harmony

Sub-Dominant Chord Family

Tonic Chord Family

Dominant Chord Family

Subdominant

| G♭ |
| IV |
| IV Maj7 |

Tonic

| D♭ |
| I |
| I Maj7 |

Leading Tone

| C |
| vii° |
| vii min7♭5 |

| A♭ |
| V |
| V Dom7 |

Dominant

| E♭ |
| ii |
| ii min7 |

Supertonic

| B♭ |
| vi |
| vi min7 |

Submediant

| F |
| iii |
| iii min7 |

Mediant

(E♭) ii° / ii min7♭5 can go to the (C) vii° / vii min7♭5

(F) iii / iii min7 can go to the (C♭) ♭VII / ♭VII Maj7 / ♭VII Dom7 **and vise versa**

(B♭) vi / vi min7 can go to the (C♭) ♭VII / ♭VII Maj7 / ♭VII Dom7 **and vise versa**

Degrees	D♭ Ionian	E♭ Dorian	F Phrygian	G♭ Lydian
Harmonized Chords	M, Madd9, Madd11, M6, Sus2, Sus4, M7sus2, M7sus4, M7	m, madd9, madd11, m6, sus2, sus4, 7sus2, 7sus4, m7	m, madd11, sus4, 7sus4, m7	M, Madd9, M6, sus2, M7sus2, M7
Borrowed Chords	I Dom7	ii° ii min7♭5	iii° iii min7♭5	iv iv min/Maj7

Degrees	A♭ Mixolydian	B♭ Aeolian	C Locrian	
Harmonized Chords	M, Madd9, Madd11, M6, sus2, sus4, 7sus2, 7sus4, 7	m, madd9, madd11, sus2, sus4, 7sus2, 7sus4, m7	dim, m7♭5	Chords built off of the Flat 7th degree are Sub-Tonic instead of Leading Tone.
Borrowed Chords	v v min7	B♭♭ ♭VI+ B♭♭ ♭VI Maj7#5	C♭ ♭VII C♭ ♭VII Maj7	C♭ ♭VII Dom7 C vii° 7

Chord Progression Chart in Key of D♭ Minor

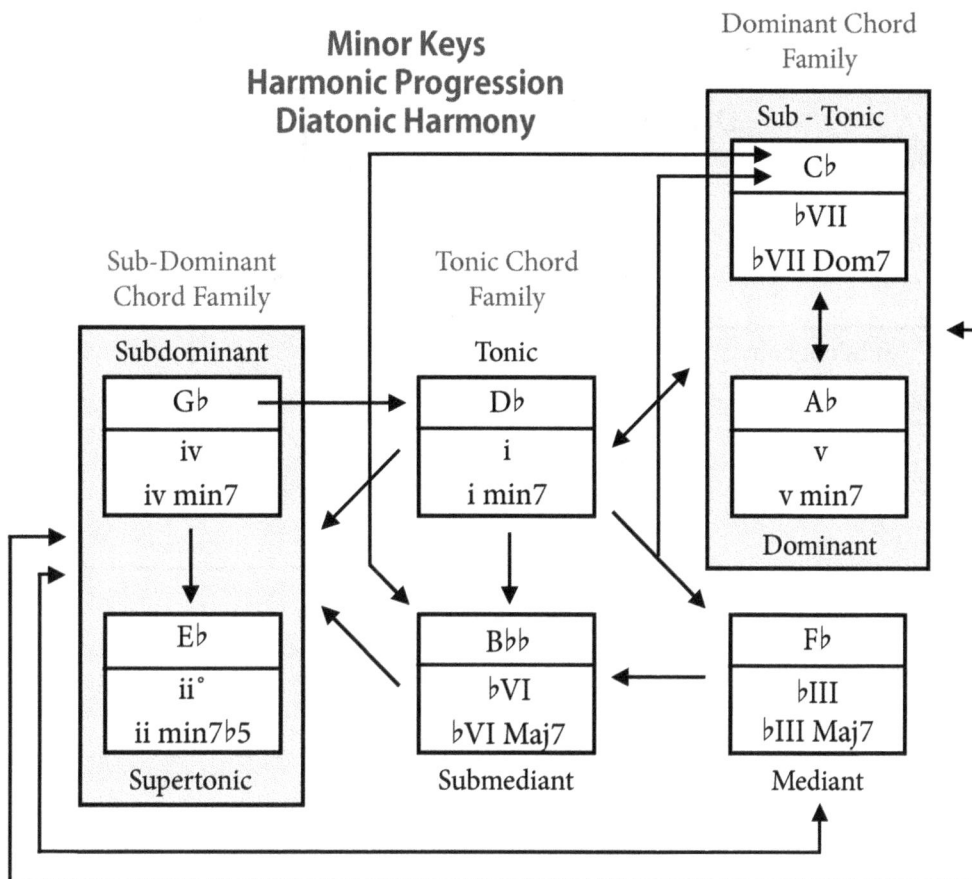

Minor Keys
Harmonic Progression
Diatonic Harmony

Dominant Chord
Family

Sub-Dominant
Chord Family

Tonic Chord
Family

Sub - Tonic

| C♭ |
| ♭VII |
| ♭VII Dom7 |

Subdominant

| G♭ |
| iv |
| iv min7 |

Tonic

| D♭ |
| i |
| i min7 |

| A♭ |
| v |
| v min7 |

Dominant

| E♭ |
| ii° |
| ii min7♭5 |

Supertonic

| B♭♭ |
| ♭VI |
| ♭VI Maj7 |

Submediant

| F♭ |
| ♭III |
| ♭III Maj7 |

Mediant

(E♭) ii° / ii min7♭5 can go to the (C) vii° / vii min7♭5

(B♭♭) ♭VI / ♭VI Maj7 can go to the (A♭) V / V Dom7 **and vise versa**

Degrees	D♭ Aeolian	E♭ Locrian	F♭ Ionian	G♭ Dorian
Harmonized Chords	m, madd9, madd11, sus2, sus4, 7sus2, 7sus4, m7	dim, m7♭5	M, Madd9, Madd11, M6, Sus2, Sus4, M7sus2, M7sus4, M7	m, madd9, madd11, m6, sus2, sus4, 7sus2, 7sus4, m7
Borrowed Chords	i min/Maj7	ii ii min7	♭III+ ♭III Maj7#5	IV IV Dom7
Degrees	A♭ Phrygian	B♭♭ Lydian	C♭ Mixolydian	
Harmonized Chords	m, madd11, sus4, 7sus4, m7	M, Madd9, M6, sus2, M7sus2, M7	M, Madd9, Madd11, M6, sus2, sus4, 7sus2, 7sus4, 7	Chords built off of the Natural 7th degree are Leading Tone instead of Sub-Tonic.
Borrowed Chords	V V Dom7	B♭ vi° B♭ vi min7♭5	C vii° C vii°7	C vii min7♭5 C♭ ♭VII Maj7

Chord Progression Chart in Key of G♭ Major

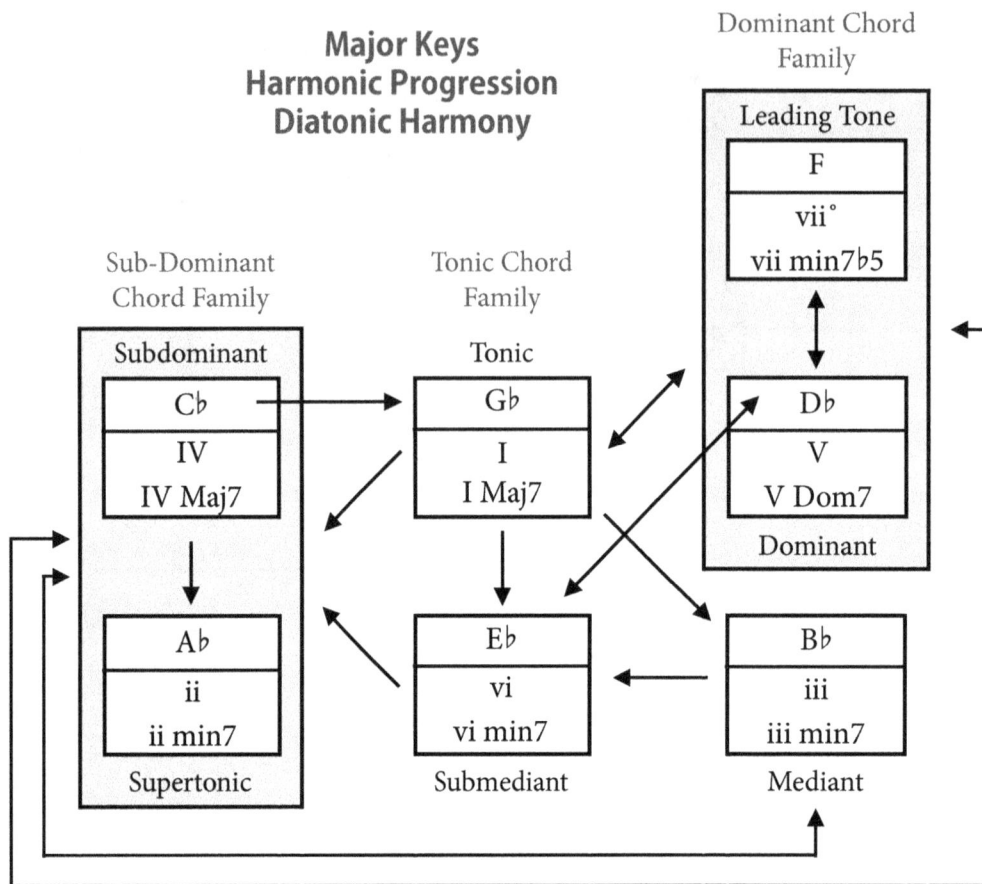

**Major Keys
Harmonic Progression
Diatonic Harmony**

Dominant Chord Family

Sub-Dominant Chord Family

Tonic Chord Family

Leading Tone
F
vii°
vii min7♭5

Subdominant
C♭
IV
IV Maj7

Tonic
G♭
I
I Maj7

D♭
V
V Dom7

Dominant

A♭
ii
ii min7

E♭
vi
vi min7

B♭
iii
iii min7

Supertonic

Submediant

Mediant

(A♭) ii° / ii min7♭5 can go to the (F) vii° / vii min7♭5

(B♭) iii / iii min7 can go to the (F♭) ♭VII / ♭VII Maj7 / ♭VII Dom7 **and vise versa**

(E♭) vi / vi min7 can go to the (F♭) ♭VII / ♭VII Maj7 / ♭VII Dom7 **and vise versa**

Degrees	G♭ Ionian	A♭ Dorian	B♭ Phrygian	C♭ Lydian
Harmonized Chords	M, Madd9, Madd11, M6, Sus2, Sus4, M7sus2, M7sus4, M7	m, madd9, madd11, m6, sus2, sus4, 7sus2, 7sus4, m7	m, madd11, sus4, 7sus4, m7	M, Madd9, M6, sus2, M7sus2, M7
Borrowed Chords	I Dom7	ii° ii min7♭5	iii° iii min7♭5	iv iv min/Maj7
Degrees	D♭ Mixolydian	E♭ Aeolian	F Locrian	
Harmonized Chords	M, Madd9, Madd11, M6, sus2, sus4, 7sus2, 7sus4, 7	m, madd9, madd11, sus2, sus4, 7sus2, 7sus4, m7	dim, m7♭5	Chords built off of the Flat 7th degree are Sub-Tonic instead of Leading Tone.
Borrowed Chords	v v min7	E♭♭ ♭VI+ E♭♭ ♭VI Maj7#5	F♭ ♭VII F♭ ♭VII Maj7	F♭ ♭VII Dom7 F vii° 7

Chord Progression Chart in Key of G♭ Minor

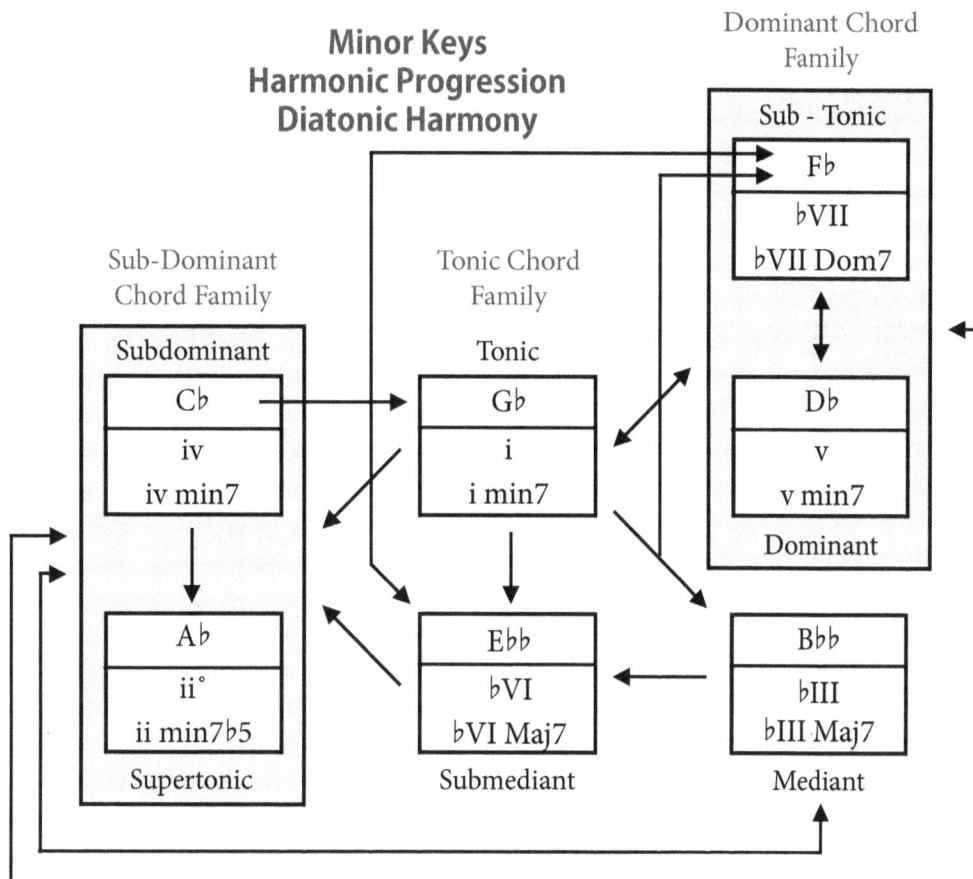

**Minor Keys
Harmonic Progression
Diatonic Harmony**

Dominant Chord
Family

Sub - Tonic
F♭
♭VII
♭VII Dom7

Sub-Dominant
Chord Family

Tonic Chord
Family

Subdominant
C♭
iv
iv min7

Tonic
G♭
i
i min7

D♭
v
v min7

Dominant

A♭
ii°
ii min7♭5

Supertonic

E♭♭
♭VI
♭VI Maj7

Submediant

B♭♭
♭III
♭III Maj7

Mediant

(A♭) ii° / ii min7♭5 can go to the (F) vii° / vii min7♭5

(E♭♭) ♭VI / ♭VI Maj7 can go to the (D♭) V / V Dom7 **and vise versa**

Degrees	G♭ Aeolian	A♭ Locrian	B♭♭ Ionian	C♭ Dorian
Harmonized Chords	m, madd9, madd11, sus2, sus4, 7sus2, 7sus4, m7	dim, m7♭5	M, Madd9, Madd11, M6, Sus2, Sus4, M7sus2, M7sus4, M7	m, madd9, madd11, m6, sus2, sus4, 7sus2, 7sus4, m7
Borrowed Chords	i min/Maj7	ii ii min7	♭III+ ♭III Maj7♯5	IV IV Dom7
Degrees	D♭ Phrygian	E♭♭ Lydian	F♭ Mixolydian	
Harmonized Chords	m, madd11, sus4, 7sus4, m7	M, Madd9, M6, sus2, M7sus2, M7	M, Madd9, Madd11, M6, sus2, sus4, 7sus2, 7sus4, 7	Chords built off of the Natural 7th degree are Leading Tone instead of Sub-Tonic.
Borrowed Chords	V V Dom7	E♭ vi° E♭ vi min7♭5	F vii° F vii°7	F vii min7♭5 F♭ ♭VII Maj7

Chord Progression Chart in Key of C♭ Major

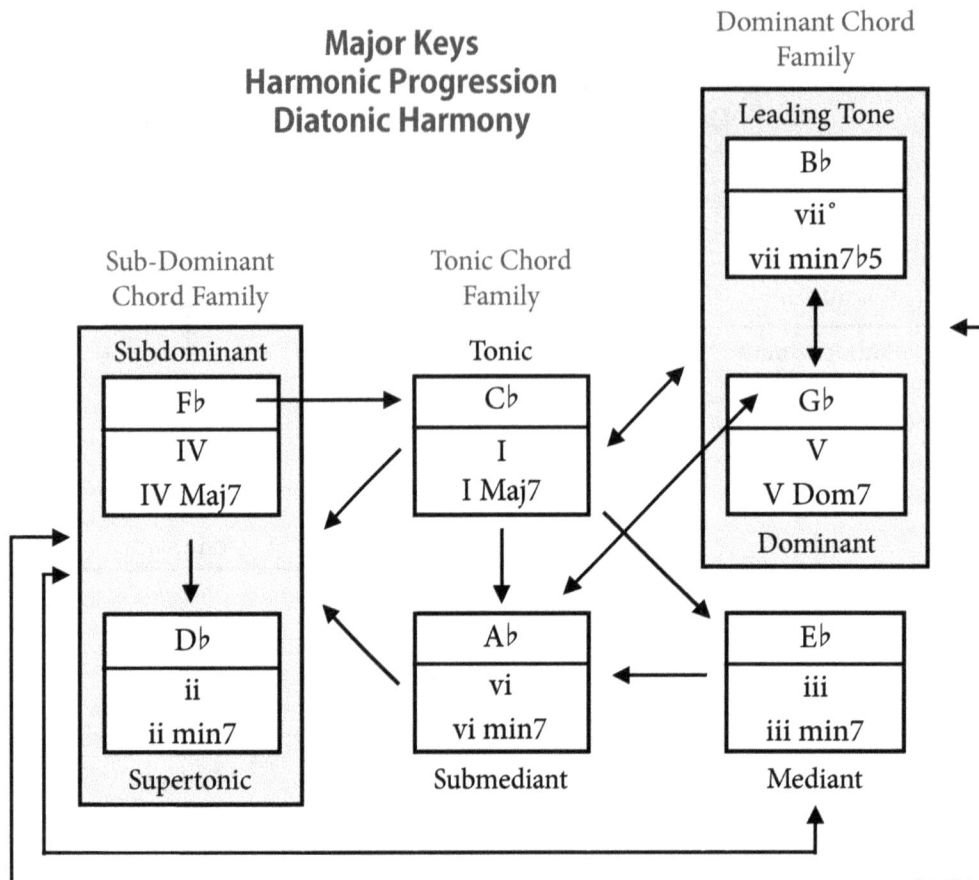

Major Keys
Harmonic Progression
Diatonic Harmony

(D♭) ii° / ii min7♭5 can go to the (B♭) vii° / vii min7♭5

(E♭) iii / iii min7 can go to the (B♭♭) ♭VII / ♭VII Maj7 / ♭VII Dom7 **and vise versa**

(A♭) vi / vi min7 can go to the (B♭♭) ♭VII / ♭VII Maj7 / ♭VII Dom7 **and vise versa**

Degrees	C♭ Ionian	D♭ Dorian	E♭ Phrygian	F♭ Lydian
Harmonized Chords	M, Madd9, Madd11, M6, Sus2, Sus4, M7sus2, M7sus4, M7	m, madd9, madd11, m6, sus2, sus4, 7sus2, 7sus4, m7	m, madd11, sus4, 7sus4, m7	M, Madd9, M6, sus2, M7sus2, M7
Borrowed Chords	I Dom7	ii° ii min7♭5	iii° iii min7♭5	iv iv min/Maj7
Degrees	G♭ Mixolydian	A♭ Aeolian	B♭ Locrian	
Harmonized Chords	M, Madd9, Madd11, M6, sus2, sus4, 7sus2, 7sus4, 7	m, madd9, madd11, sus2, sus4, 7sus2, 7sus4, m7	dim, m7♭5	Chords built off of the Flat 7th degree are Sub-Tonic instead of Leading Tone.
Borrowed Chords	v v min7	A♭♭ ♭VI+ A♭♭ ♭VI Maj7#5	B♭♭ ♭VII B♭♭ ♭VII Maj7	B♭♭ ♭VII Dom7 B♭ vii° 7

Chord Progression Chart in Key of C♭ Minor

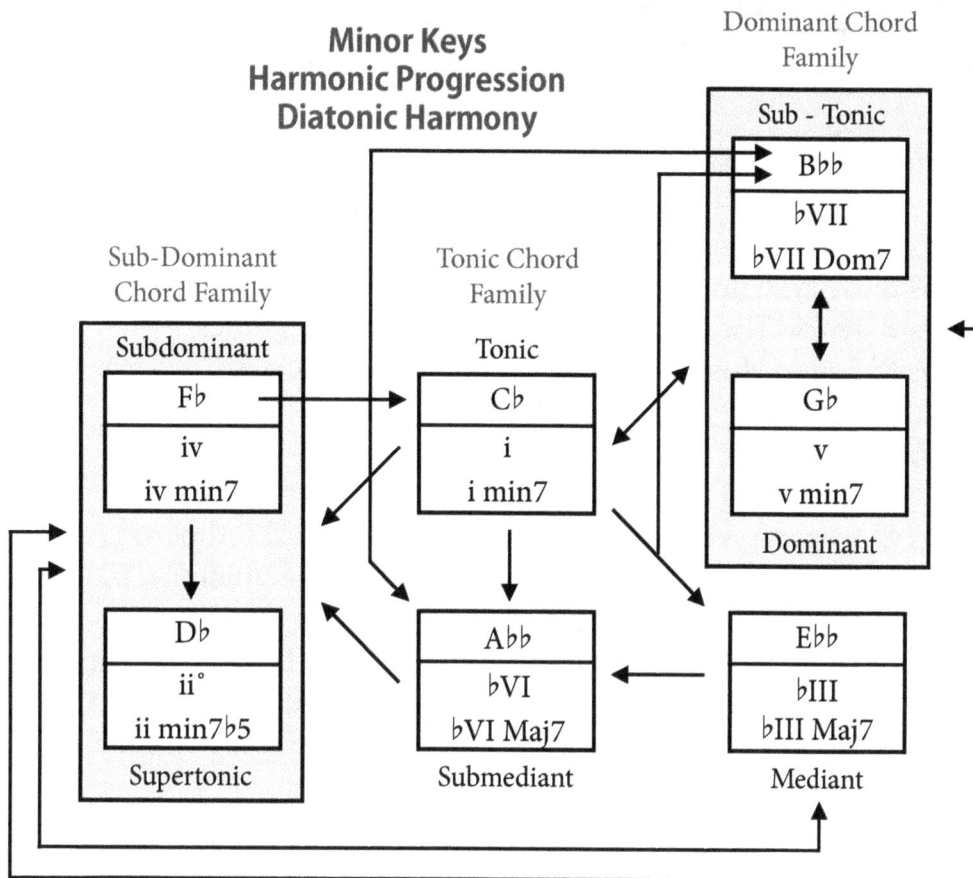

**Minor Keys
Harmonic Progression
Diatonic Harmony**

Dominant Chord Family

Sub-Dominant Chord Family

Tonic Chord Family

Sub - Tonic		
B♭♭		
♭VII		
♭VII Dom7		

Subdominant			Tonic			Gb		
F♭			C♭			G♭		
iv			i			v		
iv min7			i min7			v min7		

Dominant

D♭			A♭♭			E♭♭		
ii°			♭VI			♭III		
ii min7♭5			♭VI Maj7			♭III Maj7		

Supertonic   Submediant   Mediant

(D♭) ii° / ii min7♭5 can go to the (B♭) vii° / vii min7♭5

(A♭♭) ♭VI / ♭VI Maj7 can go to the (G♭) V / V Dom7 **and vise versa**

Degrees	C♭ Aeolian	D♭ Locrian	E♭♭ Ionian	F♭ Dorian
Harmonized Chords	m, madd9, madd11, sus2, sus4, 7sus2, 7sus4, m7	dim, m7♭5	M, Madd9, Madd11, M6, Sus2, Sus4, M7sus2, M7sus4, M7	m, madd9, madd11, m6, sus2, sus4, 7sus2, 7sus4, m7
Borrowed Chords	i min/Maj7	ii / ii min7	♭III+ / ♭III Maj7♯5	IV / IV Dom7

Degrees	G♭ Phrygian	A♭♭ Lydian	B♭♭ Mixolydian	
Harmonized Chords	m, madd11, sus4, 7sus4, m7	M, Madd9, M6, sus2, M7sus2, M7	M, Madd9, Madd11, M6, sus2, sus4, 7sus2, 7sus4, 7	Chords built off of the Natural 7th degree are Leading Tone instead of Sub-Tonic.
Borrowed Chords	V / V Dom7	A♭ vi° / A♭ vi min7♭5	B♭ vii° / B♭ vii°7	B♭ vii min7♭5 / B♭♭ ♭VII Maj7

Strings & IVORY

Check out these other titles by Strings & Ivory

1. Strings & Ivory: Chord Progressions
2. Strings & Ivory: Chords & Inversions
3. Strings & Ivory: The Exhaustive Book of Scales & Modes
4. Strings & Ivory: Music Reference Guide for Beginners

Journal books

1. Strings & Ivory: A Musicians Journal Blank Guitar Fretboard Diagrams
2. Strings & Ivory: A Musicians Journal Blank Guitar Voicinng Diagrams
3. Strings & Ivory: A Musicians Journal Blank Piano Diagrams
4. Strings & Ivory: A Musicians Journal Blank Mini Piano Diagrams
5. Strings & Ivory: A Musicians Journal Blank Chord Progression Charts
6. Strings & Ivory: A Musicians Journal Blank Step Sequence Tables

Amazon
Prints & eBooks

Draft2Digital
eBooks

Some Common Chord Progressions

I-V-vi-IV, I-IV-V, I-vi-IV-V, vi-IV-I-V, I-IV-iv-V, ii-V-I, V-IV-I, I-IV-I-V-I, I-iii-IV-V, i-V7-i-VII, III-VII-i-V7-i, i-VII-VI-V, I-II-IV-I, vi-IV-I-V, I-vi-ii-V

These are just a few examples and there are many more chord progressions. Have fun and experiment with the flow charts in the different keys found on pages 38 - 67.

Scales

Note Placement

For Guitar - The frets without notes can be either a flat note or a sharp note. For example the note between C & D can be either a C sharp or a D flat. Memorize all of the notes in the fretboard diagram below and it will be easy to know where all the sharp and flat notes are too. It will make it easy when trying to figure out where to play chords and scales.

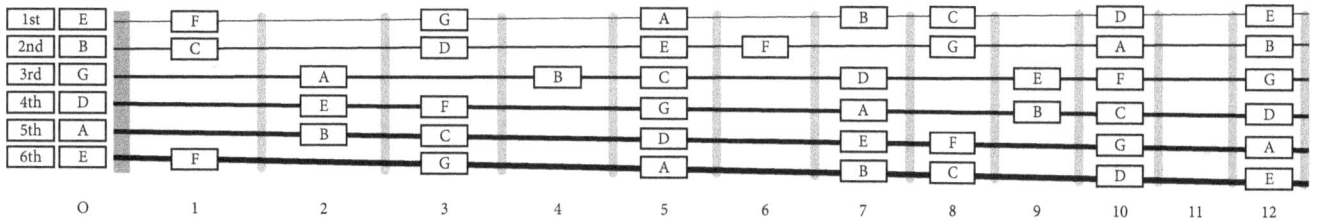

All guitar scale diagrams are in the root note C or key of C. The target notes are the root notes just like in the chord diagrams. Also just like with chords you can move the patterns up and down the neck of the guitar to change the target notes from C to any other note and the patterns will remain the same. After the 12th fret the patterns will be repeated. The 12th fret is the same as the open notes.

Ionian

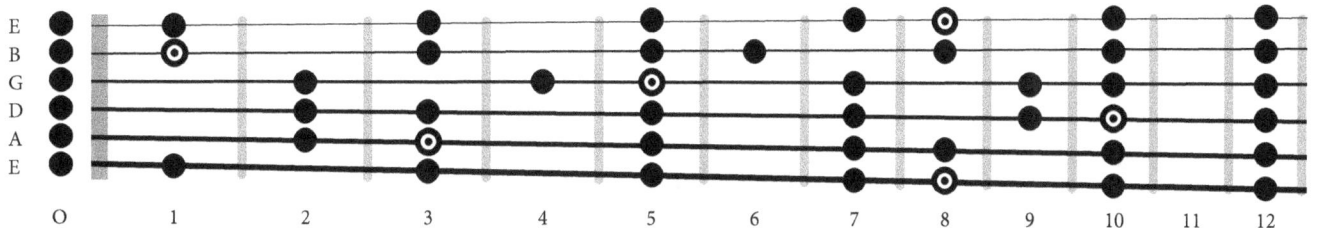

Note Placement

For Piano - All of the black keys can be either a sharp note or a flat note. For example the note between C & D can be either a C sharp or a D flat. Memorize all of the notes in the diagram below and it will be easy to know where all the sharp and flat notes are too. Every root note for the piano diagrams are included because the patterns will be different from key to key. Three ecamples below.

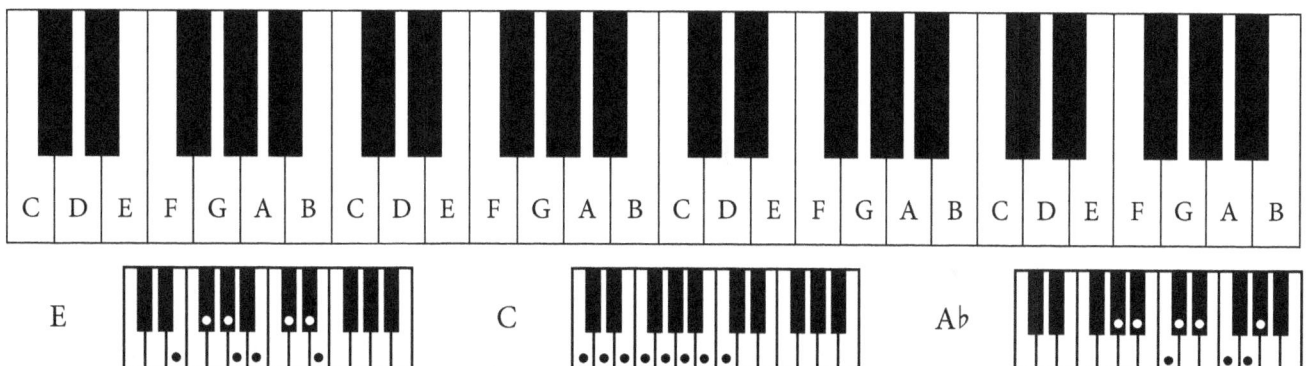

Ionian Scale (Major) Keys Chart

Keys												
	Circle of 5th's / **Circle of 4th's**											

1		2		3	4		5		6		7
C#		D#		E#	F#		G#		A#		B#
F#		G#		A#	B		C#		D#		E#
B		C#		D#	E		F#		G#		A#
E		F#		G#	A		B		C#		D#
A		B		C#	D		E		F#		G#
D		E		F#	G		A		B		C#
G		A		B	C		D		E		F#
C		D		E	F		G		A		B
F		G		A	B♭		C		D		E
B♭		C		D	E♭		F		G		A
E♭		F		G	A♭		B♭		C		D
A♭		B♭		C	D♭		E♭		F		G
D♭		E♭		F	G♭		A♭		B♭		C
G♭		A♭		B♭	C♭		D♭		E♭		F
C♭		D♭		E♭	F♭		G♭		A♭		B♭
Ionian											
1		2		3	4		5		6		7
w		w		h	w		w		w		h

Piano Scale Diagrams

E   C   A♭

A   F   C#/D♭

D   B♭   F#/G♭

G   E♭   B/C♭

Harmonic Major Scale Keys Chart

Keys (Circle of 5th's / Circle of 4th's)											
C#		D#		E#	F#		G#	A			B#
F#		G#		A#	B		C#	D			E#
B		C#		D#	E		F#	G			A#
E		F#		G#	A		B	C			D#
A		B		C#	D		E	F			G#
D		E		F#	G		A	Bb			C#
G		A		B	C		D	Eb			F#
C		D		E	F		G	Ab			B
F		G		A	Bb		C	Db			E
Bb		C		D	Eb		F	Gb			A
Eb		F		G	Ab		Bb	Cb			D
Ab		Bb		C	Db		Eb	Fb			G
Db		Eb		F	Gb		Ab	Bbb			C
Gb		Ab		Bb	Cb		Db	Ebb			F
Cb		Db		Eb	Fb		Gb	Abb			Bb

Harmonic Major

1		2		3	4		5	b6			7
	w		w		h	w		h		wh	h

Piano Scale Diagrams

E · A · D · G · C · F · Bb · Eb · Ab · C#/Db · F#/Gb · B/Cb

Hindu Scale Keys Chart

Keys

Circle of 5th's / Circle of 4th's	1		2		3	4		5	♭6		♭7	
	C#		D#		E#	F#		G#	A		B	
	F#		G#		A#	B		C#	D		E	
	B		C#		D#	E		F#	G		A	
	E		F#		G#	A		B	C		D	
	A		B		C#	D		E	F		G	
	D		E		F#	G		A	B♭		C	
	G		A		B	C		D	E♭		F	
	C		D		E	F		G	A♭		B♭	
	F		G		A	B♭		C	D♭		E♭	
	B♭		C		D	E♭		F	G♭		A♭	
	E♭		F		G	A♭		B♭	C♭		D♭	
	A♭		B♭		C	D♭		E♭	F♭		G♭	
	D♭		E♭		F	G♭		A♭	B♭♭		C♭	
	G♭		A♭		B♭	C♭		D♭	E♭♭		F♭	
	C♭		D♭		E♭	F♭		G♭	A♭♭		B♭♭	
Hindu	1		2		3	4		5	♭6		♭7	
		w		w		h		w		h	w	w

Piano Scale Diagrams

E   C   A♭

A   F   C#/D♭

D   B♭   F#/G♭

G   E♭   B/C♭

72

Mixolydian Scale Keys Chart

Keys	1		2		3	4		5		6	♭7	
C♯	C♯		D♯		E♯	F♯		G♯		A♯	B	
F♯	F♯		G♯		A♯	B		C♯		D♯	E	
B	B		C♯		D♯	E		F♯		G♯	A	
E	E		F♯		G♯	A		B		C♯	D	
A	A		B		C♯	D		E		F♯	G	
D	D		E		F♯	G		A		B	C	
G	G		A		B	C		D		E	F	
C	C		D		E	F		G		A	B♭	
F	F		G		A	B♭		C		D	E♭	
B♭	B♭		C		D	E♭		F		G	A♭	
E♭	E♭		F		G	A♭		B♭		C	D♭	
A♭	A♭		B♭		C	D♭		E♭		F	G♭	
D♭	D♭		E♭		F	G♭		A♭		B♭	C♭	
G♭	G♭		A♭		B♭	C♭		D♭		E♭	F♭	
C♭	C♭		D♭		E♭	F♭		G♭		A♭	B♭♭	
Mixolydian	1		2		3	4		5		6	♭7	
		w		w		h	w		w		h	w

Keys: Circle of 5th's / Circle of 4th's

Piano Scale Diagrams

E   C   A♭

A   F   C♯/D♭

D   B♭   F♯/G♭

G   E♭   B/C♭

73

Aeolian Scale (Natural Minor) Keys Chart

Keys											
C#		D#	E		F#		G#	A		B	
F#		G#	A		B		C#	D		E	
B		C#	D		E		F#	G		A	
E		F#	G		A		B	C		D	
A		B	C		D		E	F		G	
D		E	F		G		A	Bb		C	
G		A	Bb		C		D	Eb		F	
C		D	Eb		F		G	Ab		Bb	
F		G	Ab		Bb		C	Db		Eb	
Bb		C	Db		Eb		F	Gb		Ab	
Eb		F	Gb		Ab		Bb	Cb		Db	
Ab		Bb	Cb		Db		Eb	Fb		Gb	
Db		Eb	Fb		Gb		Ab	Bbb		Cb	
Gb		Ab	Bbb		Cb		Db	Ebb		Fb	
Cb		Db	Ebb		Fb		Gb	Abb		Bbb	
Aeolian 1		2	b3		4		5	b6		b7	
w	h	w		w		w	h	w		w	

Circle of 5th's
Circle of 4th's

Piano Scale Diagrams

E

A

D

G

C

F

Bb

Eb

Ab

C#/Db

F#/Gb

B/Cb

Harmonic Minor Scale Keys Chart

Keys	1		2	b3		4		5	b6			7
Circle of 5ths / Circle of 4ths	C#		D#	E		F#		G#	A			B#
	F#		G#	A		B		C#	D			E#
	B		C#	D		E		F#	G			A#
	E		F#	G		A		B	C			D#
	A		B	C		D		E	F			G#
	D		E	F		G		A	Bb			C#
	G		A	Bb		C		D	Eb			F#
	C		D	Eb		F		G	Ab			B
	F		G	Ab		Bb		C	Db			E
	Bb		C	Db		Eb		F	Gb			A
	Eb		F	Gb		Ab		Bb	Cb			D
	Ab		Bb	Cb		Db		Eb	Fb			G
	Db		Eb	Fb		Gb		Ab	Bbb			C
	Gb		Ab	Bbb		Cb		Db	Ebb			F
	Cb		Db	Ebb		Fb		Gb	Abb			Bb
Harmonic Minor	1		2	b3		4		5	b6			7
	w	h	w		w	h		wh		h		

Piano Scale Diagrams

E, A, D, G, C, F, Bb, Eb, Ab, C#/Db, F#/Gb, B/Cb

Melodic Minor Scale Keys Chart

Keys — Circle of 5th's / Circle of 4th's

1	2	b3	4	5	6	7
C#	D#	E	F#	G#	A#	B#
F#	G#	A	B	C#	D#	E#
B	C#	D	E	F#	G#	A#
E	F#	G	A	B	C#	D#
A	B	C	D	E	F#	G#
D	E	F	G	A	B	C#
G	A	Bb	C	D	E	F#
C	D	Eb	F	G	A	B
F	G	Ab	Bb	C	D	E
Bb	C	Db	Eb	F	G	A
Eb	F	Gb	Ab	Bb	C	D
Ab	Bb	Cb	Db	Eb	F	G
Db	Eb	Fb	Gb	Ab	Bb	C
Gb	Ab	Bbb	Cb	Db	Eb	F
Cb	Db	Ebb	Fb	Gb	Ab	Bb

Melodic Minor

1	2	b3	4	5	6	7
w	h	w	w	w	w	h

Piano Scale Diagrams

E   C   Ab

A   F   C#/Db

D   Bb   F#/Gb

G   Eb   B/Cb

Dorian Scale Keys Chart

Keys — Circle of 5th's / Circle of 4th's

1		2	♭3		4		5		6	♭7	
C#		D#	E		F#		G#		A#	B	
F#		G#	A		B		C#		D#	E	
B		C#	D		E		F#		G#	A	
E		F#	G		A		B		C#	D	
A		B	C		D		E		F#	G	
D		E	F		G		A		B	C	
G		A	B♭		C		D		E	F	
C		D	E♭		F		G		A	B♭	
F		G	A♭		B♭		C		D	E♭	
B♭		C	D♭		E♭		F		G	A♭	
E♭		F	G♭		A♭		B♭		C	D♭	
A♭		B♭	C♭		D♭		E♭		F	G♭	
D♭		E♭	F♭		G♭		A♭		B♭	C♭	
G♭		A♭	B♭♭		C♭		D♭		E♭	F♭	
C♭		D♭	E♭♭		F♭		G♭		A♭	B♭♭	
Dorian 1		2	♭3		4		5		6	♭7	
	w	h		w		w		w	h		w

Piano Scale Diagrams

E, A, D, G

C, F, B♭, E♭

A♭, C#/D♭, F#/G♭, B/C♭

Major Pentatonic Blues Scale Keys Chart

Keys (Circle of 5th's / Circle of 4th's)	1		2	b3	3			5	6		
C#	C#		D#	E	E#			G#	A#		
F#	F#		G#	A	A#			C#	D#		
B	B		C#	D	D#			F#	G#		
E	E		F#	G	G#			B	C#		
A	A		B	C	C#			E	F#		
D	D		E	F	F#			A	B		
G	G		A	Bb	B			D	E		
C	C		D	Eb	E			G	A		
F	F		G	Ab	A			C	D		
Bb	Bb		C	Db	D			F	G		
Eb	Eb		F	Gb	G			Bb	C		
Ab	Ab		Bb	Cb	C			Eb	F		
Db	Db		Eb	Fb	F			Ab	Bb		
Gb	Gb		Ab	Bbb	Bb			Db	Eb		
Cb	Cb		Db	Ebb	Eb			Gb	Ab		
Major Pent. Blues	1		2	b3	3			5	6		
		w		h		h	wh		w		wh

Piano Scale Diagrams

E   C   Ab

A   F   C#/Db

D   Bb   F#/Gb

G   Eb   B/Cb

Minor Pentatonic Blues Scale Keys Chart

		1			b3		4	b5	5			b7	
Circle of 5th's → Circle of 4th's	Keys	C#			E		F#	G	G#			B	
		F#			A		B	C	C#			E	
		B			D		E	F	F#			A	
		E			G		A	Bb	B			D	
		A			C		D	Eb	E			G	
		D			F		G	Ab	A			C	
		G			Bb		C	Db	D			F	
		C			Eb		F	Gb	G			Bb	
		F			Ab		Bb	Cb	C			Eb	
		Bb			Db		Eb	Fb	F			Ab	
		Eb			Gb		Ab	Bbb	Bb			Db	
		Ab			Cb		Db	Ebb	Eb			Gb	
		Db			Fb		Gb	Abb	Ab			Cb	
		Gb			Bbb		Cb	Dbb	Db			Fb	
		Cb			Ebb		Fb	Gbb	Gb			Bbb	
Minor Pent. Blues		1			b3		4	b5	5			b7	

	wh		w		h	h		wh		w

Piano Scale Diagrams

E   C   Ab

A   F   C#/Db

D   Bb   F#/Gb

G   Eb   B/Cb

Major Pentatonic Scale Keys Chart

Keys					
C#	D#	E#		G#	A#
F#	G#	A#		C#	D#
B	C#	D#		F#	G#
E	F#	G#		B	C#
A	B	C#		E	F#
D	E	F#		A	B
G	A	B		D	E
C	D	E		G	A
F	G	A		C	D
Bb	C	D		F	G
Eb	F	G		Bb	C
Ab	Bb	C		Eb	F
Db	Eb	F		Ab	Bb
Gb	Ab	Bb		Db	Eb
Cb	Db	Eb		Gb	Ab

Keys — Circle of 5th's — Circle of 4th's

Major Pentatonic	1	2	3		5	6	
	w		w		wh	w	wh

Piano Scale Diagrams

E, A, D, G

C, F, Bb, Eb

Ab, C#/Db, F#/Gb, B/Cb

Minor Pentatonic Scale Keys Chart

Keys	1		b3	4	5		b7	
C#	C#		E	F#	G#		B	
F#	F#		A	B	C#		E	
B	B		D	E	F#		A	
E	E		G	A	B		D	
A	A		C	D	E		G	
D	D		F	G	A		C	
G	G		Bb	C	D		F	
C	C		Eb	F	G		Bb	
F	F		Ab	Bb	C		Eb	
Bb	Bb		Db	Eb	F		Ab	
Eb	Eb		Gb	Ab	Bb		Db	
Ab	Ab		Cb	Db	Eb		Gb	
Db	Db		Fb	Gb	Ab		Cb	
Gb	Gb		Bbb	Cb	Db		Fb	
Cb	Cb		Ebb	Fb	Gb		Bbb	
Minor Pentatonic	1		b3	4	5		b7	
		wh		w	w		wh	w

Circle of 5th's — Circle of 4th's

Piano Scale Diagrams

Guitar Scale Diagrams

Ionian
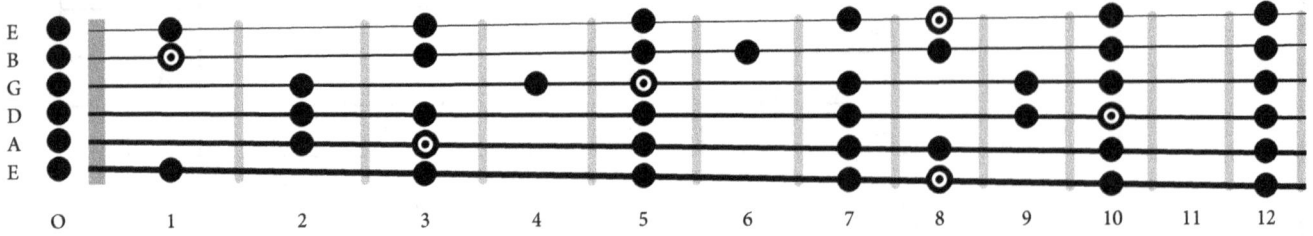

Harmonic Major
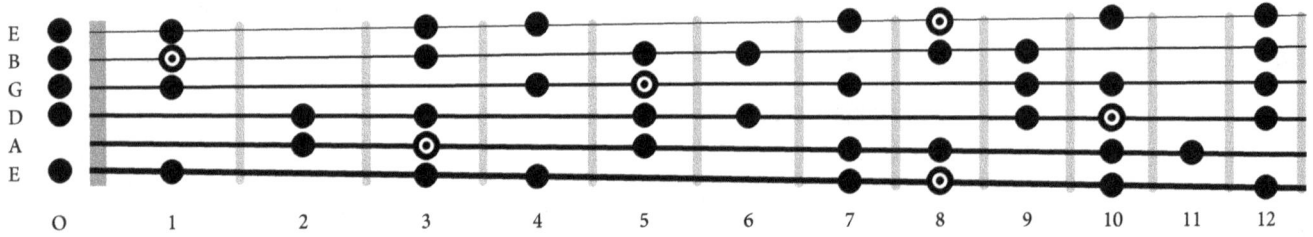

Hindu
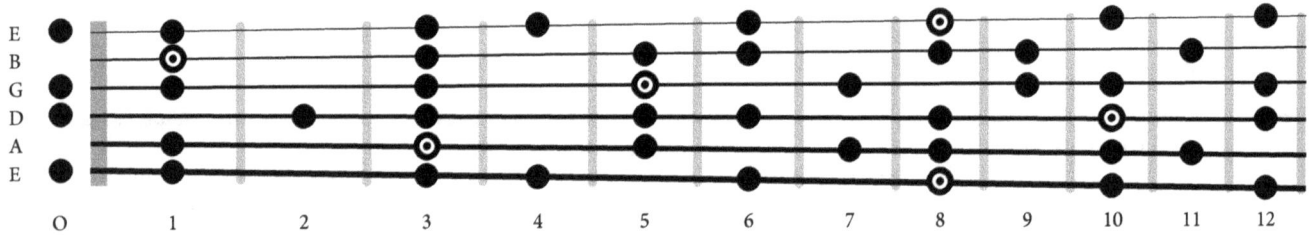

Mixolydian
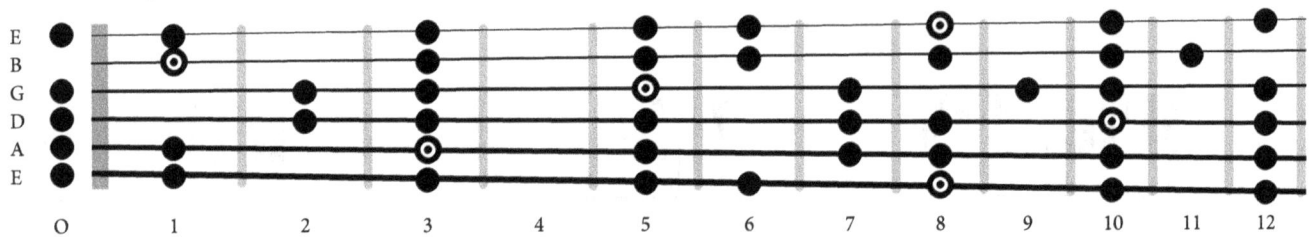

Aeolian
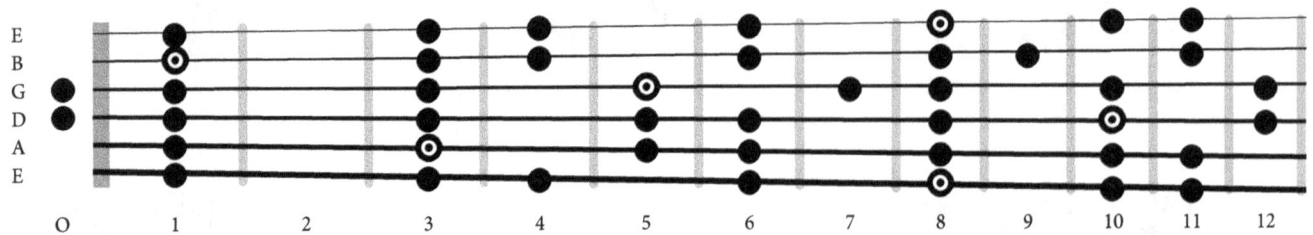

Harmonic Minor
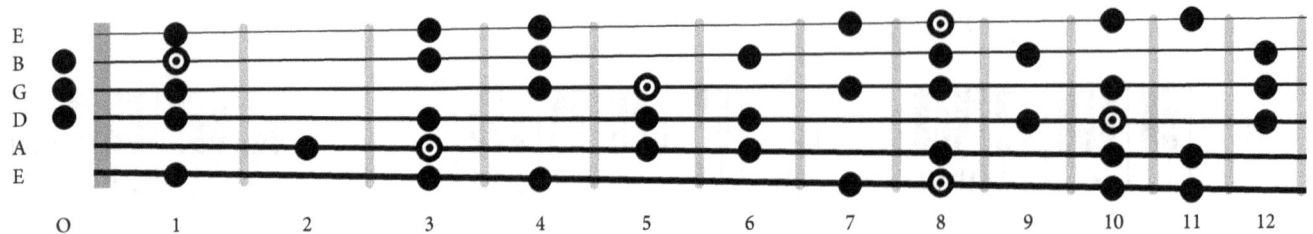

Guitar Scale Diagrams

Melodic Minor

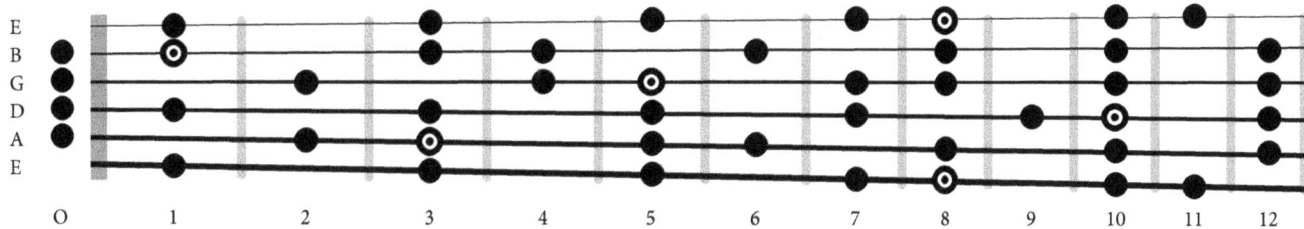

Dorian

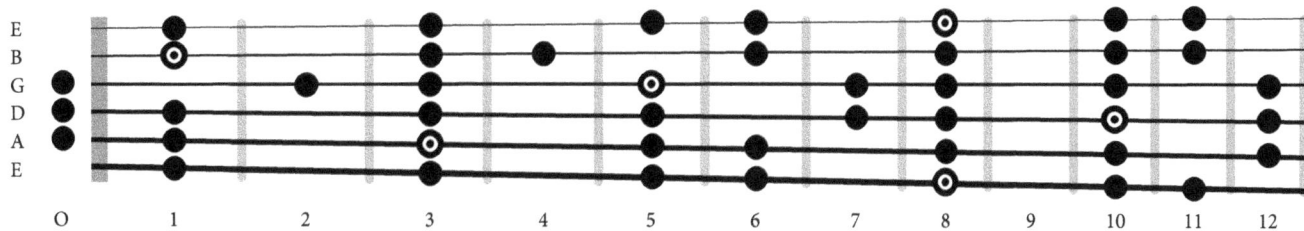

Major Pent. Blues

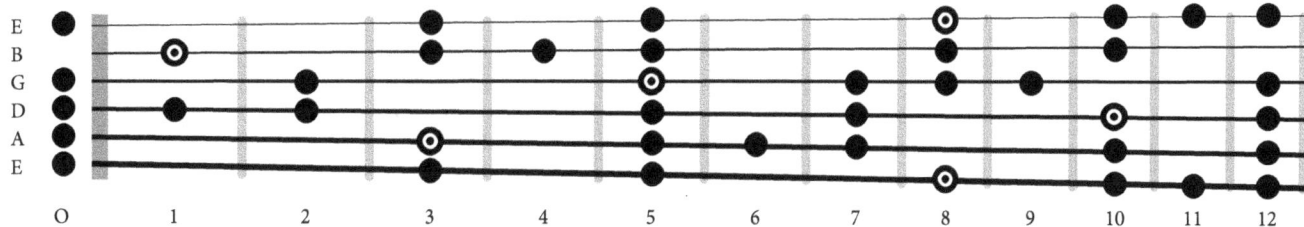

Minor Pent. Blues

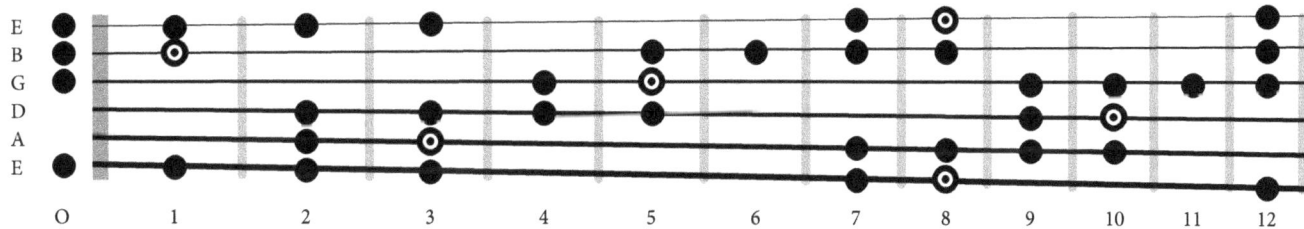

Major Pentatonic

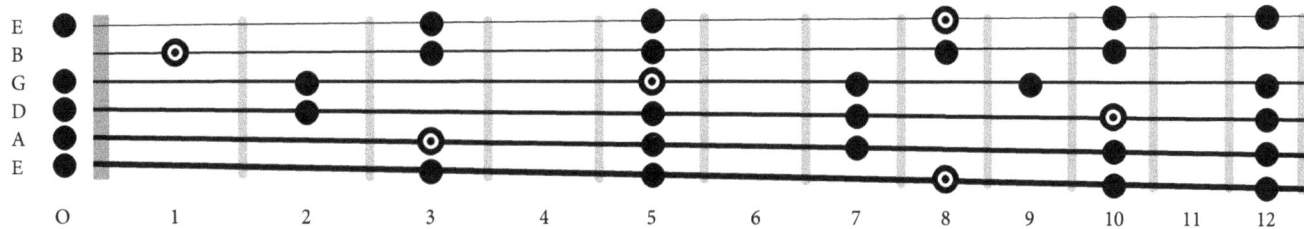

Minor Pentatonic

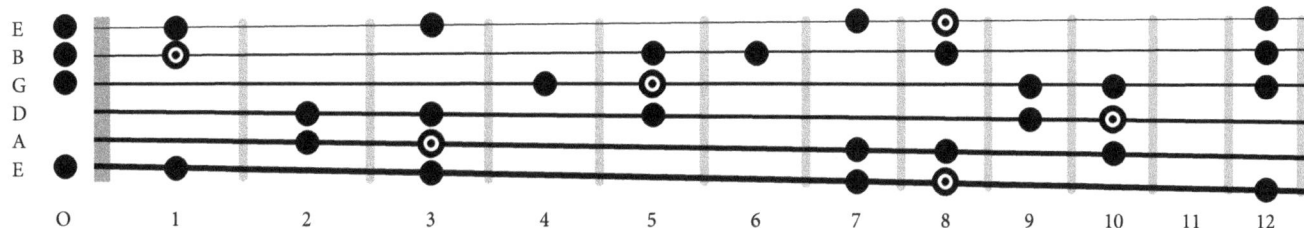

www.ingramcontent.com/pod-product-compliance
Lightning Source LLC
Chambersburg PA
CBHW080602030426
42336CB00019B/3298